I0140241

Theologia Viatorum
Vol. 1 No. 1

Theologia Viatorum: The Journal of the London Lyceum

Published in the United States of America by Hanover Press

©The London Lyceum 2023

All rights reserved. No part of this publication may be reproduced, stored in a retrieval system, or transmitted, in any form or by any means, without the prior permission in writing of The London Lyceum, or as expressly permitted by law, by license, or under terms agreed with the appropriate reproduction rights organization.

Email: contact@thelondonlyceum.com

Website: www.thelondonlyceum.com

Paperback ISBN: 979-8-9881179-0-2

Theologia Viatorum

Theologia Viatorum (theology of the pilgrims) is a peer-reviewed journal for analytic, Baptist, and/or confessional theology that is published on an annual basis by Hanover Press, the publishing house of the London Lyceum. The journal seeks to promote serious thinking for a serious church by retrieving the wisdom from analytic philosophy, the Baptist tradition, and classical Protestantism as confessed in the confessional documents of the Reformed tradition. The journal seeks to promote the Reformed catholic tradition by confessing what is held in common by the Second London Confession of Faith, the Orthodox Creed (1679), the Westminster Confession of Faith, the Three Forms of Unity, and the Anglican Formularies. The journal publishes content that confesses the Nicene and Apostles' Creed and is consistent with the orthodox Protestant confessional tradition.

Articles that deal with analytic theology, Baptist theology, or confessional theology are very welcome. However, any theological or philosophical article advancing serious Christian thinking is welcome as well.

EDITORS

Jordan L. Steffaniak, Editor
The London Lyceum

Garrett M. Walden, Senior Editor
Grace Heritage Church

Brandon Ayscue, Associate Editor
Harriett Baptist Church

Christopher Woznicki, Associate Editor of Analytic Theology
Fuller Theological Seminary

Morgan Byrd, Associate Editor of Confessional Theology
Palmetto Shores Church

Cody Floate, Associate Editor of Exegetical Theology
Puritan Reformed Theological Seminary

Conner McMakin, Associate Editor of Pastoral Theology
First Baptist Church of Spring Lake

Jake Stone, Associate Editor of Baptist Theology
The Southern Baptist Theological Seminary

Hunter Hindsman, Book Review Editor
The Southern Baptist Theological Seminary

EDITORIAL BOARD

Guillaume Bignon, PhD (Association Axiome)

Jason Alligood, PhD (Fellowship Bible Church)

Benjamin Quinn, PhD (Southeastern Baptist Theological Seminary)

Geoff Chang, PhD (Midwestern Baptist Theological Seminary)

James Anderson, PhD (Reformed Theological Seminary)

J.T. Turner, PhD (Anderson University)

Mitch Chase, PhD (Kosmosdale Baptist Church)

David Hogg, PhD (Phoenix Seminary)

Brandon D. Smith, PhD (Cedarville University)

Matthew C. Bingham, PhD (Oak Hill College)

Jesse Owens, PhD (Welch College)

Contents

Theologia Viatorum: The Journal of The London Lyceum

Vol. 1 No. 1, March 2023

Editorial

I am very proud to introduce the inaugural issue of *Theologia Viatorum: The Journal of the London Lyceum*. *Theologia Viatorum* is Latin for theology of the pilgrims which well encapsulates our journey toward God in this life. We are but humble pilgrims, dependent upon divine grace, striving for the beatific vision and restoration of the cosmos.

In this first issue on the liberty of conscience, we have the honor of publishing articles from Garrett Walden, James Renihan, Jesse Owens, Joseph Dunne, Geoff Chang, and J. Ryan Davidson. Each of these men have provided careful essays that should be of great interest to all. The issue also includes a fascinating special essay introduced, edited, and transcribed by Jordan Senécal. Finally, four of the most popular book reviews for our website at the London Lyceum have been re-published here in print for wider circulation. The London Lyceum has always been about serious thinking for a serious church and I'm convinced the essays herein will serve this end.

Many hours of sweat were poured into this first issue and it's only a matter of divine grace that the issue has seen fit to be completed. Numerous people ought to be thanked, especially our Senior Editor Garrett Walden, who not only submitted his own article for double-blind peer review but has assisted in editing our content with painstaking detail. Further thanks go to the many blind reviewers who have been willing to assist us in our venture to begin an academic journal that is of the highest quality. Not only have they insisted on the highest quality, but they have been punctual, completing reviews in record time. Finally, incredible thanks go to Isabella Sabatier for her selfless and tireless work to assist with the typesetting of our first issue, which is no easy feat. She will be rewarded by our Lord who takes notice of every deed done both in public and in secret. It was by divine appointment that I mentioned our need for assistance with typesetting to her husband Lucas who volunteered her assistance with our project. Praise is due to our God who meticulously orders our every movement.

Jordan L. Steffaniak

President and Editor

Robert Robinson's Liberty:
Toleration, Conscience, and Ecclesiology

Garrett M. Walden, ThM

Baptists have long been champions of religious freedom and toleration, often by necessity and under duress. From their beginnings Baptists have "sensed that freedom in Christ was not only freedom to hear and receive the Gospel, but above all freedom to interpret Scripture and to believe according to the way, under God, one was directed by conscience."[1] It was this sensibility, and some particular interpretive decisions along with it, that led to the emergence of the Baptists, though their early history was fraught with opposition.

In the tumult of the Enlightenment in the long eighteenth century, Robert Robinson (1735-1790) was a Particular Baptist pastor in Cambridge, England.[2] Robinson was born in Norfolk where he gained a limited education. At fourteen he became a barber's apprentice in London. In May of 1752, he heard George Whitefield preach, and the sermon haunted him for three years until his conversion in December of 1755. He shortly thereafter became a Methodist minister, but in 1759 he changed his view to believer's baptism by immersion. In 1761, through the assistance of Anne Dutton and a recommendation by John Gill, he was called to be the pastor of the Stoneyard congregation, a Baptist church in Cambridge.[3] Smith notes that "Robinson's sermons were characterized by a warm, evangelical Calvinism in which he invited people to embrace the Gospel and receive freedom and redemption offered by God."[4] In his early days as pastor of the weak church, he was vigilant and rigorous in church discipline and in catechizing the anemic believers

---

1   Karen Smith, "The Liberty Not to Be a Christian: Robert Robinson (1735-1790) of Cambridge and Freedom of Conscience," in *Distinctively Baptist: Essays on Baptist History. A Festschrift in Honor of Walter B. Shurden*, ed. Marc A. Jolley and John D. Pierce (Macon, GA: Mercer University Press, 2005), 151.
2   Colin McGahey notes that "Robinson was deeply studious of the work of both Milton and Locke, which undoubtedly spurred his interest in government as well as natural law." See Colin M. McGahey, "Transcriber's Preface to Slavery Inconsistent with the Spirit of Christianity: An 18th Century Baptist Advocates Freedom," *Southwestern Journal of Theology* 48, no. 2 (Spring 2006), 218.
3   McGahey, "Transcriber's Preface," 216.
4   Smith, "The Liberty Not to Be a Christian," 154.

there. Over time, the church experienced remarkable growth and health.[5] He pastored in Cambridge till his death in 1790, but his ministry was plagued with controversy, both inside and outside the Baptist denomination. All along the way, "his political views caused strife among some members of his church," (for instance, his support of both the American and French Revolutions), and he frequently received calls for resignation.[6]

In this essay, I will analyze the argument of Robinson's treatise *The General Doctrine of Toleration Applied to the Particular Case of Free Communion.*[7] As a leading voice in "the communion controversy" of his day, he wrote this fifty-page essay in 1781 to make a case for theological latitude on the fencing of the Lord's Table, but he expresses a larger hermeneutic for dealing with theological differences. While I personally differ from Robinson's conclusion on the open-versus-strict communion question, I find his argument to be the best version of the open position because of his careful and powerful rhetoric without sacrificing clear argumentation. My purpose here is not to seek to disprove his position, but to hold him up as a strong defender of the idea of intra-ecclesial toleration. Therefore, after re-presenting his case, I will point to some insights for contemporary application before I conclude with a word of warning from Robinson's life and ministry.

1. The General Doctrine of Toleration

What sort of agreement is to be expected in the church? From the outset, Robinson distinguishes between "unity of faith" and "uniformity of practice," by which he means the content of biblical doctrine and the different modes of expression of that shared content. He notes that Roman Catholics, Reformed, and Nonconformist churches have used various means to try to hold the two together. Robinson admits that keeping the two together across multiple congregations is unattainable, and so churches must be constituted "to allow variety of sentiment and practice."[8] However, he acknowledges that

---

5   Thomas R. McKibbens records that Robinson "attracted crowds of six to seven hundred people two and sometimes three times each Sunday, and required the building of a new sanctuary to seat the weekly throngs." (Thomas R. McKibbens, Jr. "Robert Robinson: Baptist Historian with a Passion for Preaching" *Baptist History and Heritage* 15, no. 4 [October 1980], 12.)
6   McGahey, "Transcriber's Preface," 217.
7   Robert Robinson, *The General Doctrine of Toleration Applied to the Particular Case of Free Communion* (Cambridge: Hodson, 1781), 3. A number of other works by Robinson would be relevant to this discussion as well, for example his *Arcana, or, The Principles of the Late Petitioners to Parliament for Relief in the Matter of Subscription: in VIII. Letters to a Friend* (Cambridge: Hodson, 1773). Also, his *Reflections on Christian Liberty, Civil Establishments of Religion, and Toleration* (Harlow, UK: B. Flower, 1805), not to mention many relevant letters and sermons.
8   Robinson, *The General Doctrine of Toleration*, 3. Smith notes that, "Robinson realized that if people were urged to study Scripture and to follow their conscience, inevitably there would

Christian liberty in faith and practice must remain within certain bounds, so that it does not "run into licentiousness, as it would if it went so far as to hazard the purity of gospel worship and order."[9]

1.1 Robinson's Recounting of the History

To bolster his thesis that believer's baptism by immersion should not be a criterion for participation in the Lord's Supper, Robinson recounts the history of "the communion controversy," which has been well summarized more recently in Peter Naylor's book, *Calvinism, Communion, and the Baptists*.[10] For Robinson, the controversy emerged in 1633 when the London pastors John Spilsbury (1593–1668) and John Lathrop (1584–1653) split over the question of infant baptism. In 1638, William Kiffen (1616–1701) came into conflict with Spilsbury over whether a person not baptized by immersion may preach. Taking the negative view, Kiffen left with his congregation. From there the logic extended to barring from the Supper those not baptized by immersion as professing believers. Robinson identifies Kiffen's later essay, *A Sober Discourse of Right to Church Communion* (1681) to be "the first piece published professedly on this subject."[11] This is a strange comment because he then says that Henry Jessey (1603–1663) took the side of "mixt communion" and wrote on the topic before his death in 1663. Then, of course, John Bunyan (1628–1688) wrote his confession of faith in 1672, which "pleaded warmly for mixt communion."[12] This ignited the famous pamphlet war of the mid-1670s between Kiffen and Bunyan, and Robinson adjudicates the debate and offers a sarcastic remark or two.

The debate subsided for a while before it was reignited again in the 1750s when James Foster (1697–1753) published a sermon entitled *Catholic Communion*, defending mixed communion. A layman, Grantham Killingworth (1699–1778), responded in opposition. In 1772, Daniel Turner (1710–1798) of Abingdon, John C. Ryland (1723–1792) of Northampton, and John Brown (d. 1800) of Kettering took up the mixed communion side against James Turner

---

be differences of opinion. For him, more important than unity of opinion was the right to read Scripture and with the help of God as Holy Spirit to interpret for oneself the meaning of the word." (Smith, "The Liberty Not to Be a Christian," 161.)

9   Robinson, *The General Doctrine of Toleration*, 4.

10   Peter Naylor, *Calvinism, Communion, and the Baptists: A Study of English Calvinistic Baptists from the Late 1600s to the Early 1800s*, Studies in Baptist History and Thought 7 (Eugene, OR: Wipf & Stock, 2006). It is unusual that Naylor speaks only tangentially of Robinson, but never engages any of Robinson's work or historical significance.

11   Robinson, *The General Doctrine of Toleration*, 5.

12   Robinson, *The General Doctrine of Toleration*, 6.

of Birmingham, Abraham Booth (1726–1780) of London, and William Buttfield (d. 1778) of Thorn (among other pseudonymous authors on both sides).

This is the history of the Baptist debate of the communion controversy up to the point of Robinson's essay, and Robinson notes that one of the reasons he loves Baptist church polity is:

> Because it admits of free debate…that can produce a dispute of one hundred and fifty years unstained with the blood, and unsullied with the fines, the imprisonments and the civil inconveniences of the disputants. As to a few coarse names, rough compliments, foreign suppositions, and acrimonious exclamations, they are only the harmless squeakings of men in a passion caught and pinched in a sort of logical trap.[13]

From here he excuses the "squeakings" and attends to the substance of the debate, under the headings of "a case of fact" and "a case of right," before drawing his conclusion.

1.2 A Case of Fact

The "case of fact" is Robinson's acknowledgement that it is simply *a fact* that people believe different things about the question of the proper participants in the Supper. He writes:

> Many sincere disciples of Christ declare, that, having renounced all authority except that of the holy scriptures, to decide in all matters of faith and practice, and having searched the scriptures with all the diligence and rectitude, of which they are capable, they think infant baptism of divine appointment, and rightly performed by sprinkling water on the face.

Further, it is simply *a fact* that there are some Baptist churches that "do conscientiously admit such persons into their fellowship," with no disruption.[14] Robinson states that he has pastored such a mixed church for twenty years with no disadvantage.

However, it is also *a fact* that since the emergence of the Baptists in England, "many have refused, and to this day continue to refuse to admit into their fellowship all manner of persons, however qualified in other respects, who have not been baptized by immersion on their own profession of faith and repentance." These stricter Baptist churches readily acknowledge

---

13 Robinson, *The General Doctrine of Toleration*, 8.
14 Robinson, *The General Doctrine of Toleration*, 9.

the Christian profession of these unbaptized believers and "account them members of the mystical body of Christ," yet nevertheless refuse to admit them to church fellowship. Because Baptists do not believe baptism by immersion to be "a saving ordinance nor do they think it a test of true religion, nor do they hold that unbaptized believers ought not to be tolerated in a state, nor do they deny any intelligent being the right of private judgment," therefore, "they only refuse to tolerate infant baptism in their own churches."[15]

As a final point of *fact*, Robinson asserts that "the primitive churches, those in Greece, that at Rome, and all others, were originally constituted baptist churches, and that they lost the ordinances of baptism, along with the doctrines of the gospel, and the very nature and essence of christian churches."[16] In his assessment, this happened not because they were too tolerant of reasonable differences, but because they prioritized "certain external qualifications of church members, which in time became tests of orthodoxy, to which wicked men could and did conform, under pretence of authority from Christ to establish uniformity."[17] In his view, these are simply the facts, and Christians should distinguish what *is* from what *ought to be*, which leads neatly into his "case of right."

1.3 A Case of Right

Robinson's "case of right" centers on the question: "What makes it just and right for churches to admit of mixt communion?" His answer boils down to: "the revealed will of Jesus Christ."[18] If only that settled the matter! To defend his answer, Robinson first rules out many authorities as proper sources of judgment on the matter of church fellowship. He rules out the early church fathers, the Reformed scholastics, the Puritans, and even New Testament examples because there is no proper parallel in their time since credobaptists and paedobaptists were not overlapping. He also rules out appeals to Roman Catholics and non-Christian scholars since the former are bound to papal authority which Protestants do not recognize, and the latter have no jurisdiction or interest in church affairs.[19] For Robinson, appealing to these sources is a manipulative tactic to overwhelm the uneducated and

---

15 Robinson, *The General Doctrine of Toleration*, 10.
16 Robinson, *The General Doctrine of Toleration*, 11. This is an extraordinary claim, which he defends and develops in his magnum opus, *The History of Baptism* (London: Couchman and Fry, 1790).
17 Robinson, *The General Doctrine of Toleration*, 11.
18 Robinson, *The General Doctrine of Toleration*, 12.
19 Robinson, *The General Doctrine of Toleration*, 12–13.

common Baptist church member. Surprisingly, Robinson also rules out appeals to prominent Baptist thinkers and writers, because for every name one could cite in favor of one view, an opponent could cite a name of similar reputation in favor of the contrary view. In other words, Robinson believes historical Baptist sources are evenly split in the number of works, strength of argument, and reputation of the authors. Furthermore, he believes Baptist polity sides against appeals even to intra-traditional sources, since no Baptist minister or church can wield any formal authority over the doctrine and practice of another congregation.

Continuing, Robinson rules out appeals to natural instincts or "general notions of benevolence and usefulness," because the constitution and operations of the church are to be regulated only by Scripture.[20] Pragmatism and politeness should not sway the conversation. Finally, he rules out appeals to "accidental circumstances" to determine the question.[21] By accidental circumstances, he has in mind quirks of personality that may hinder the persuasiveness of an argument, honest but unintentional mistakes and self-contradictions, and slippery-slope arguments that might lead to "frightful consequences." He thus concludes that "the right or wrong of this case is determinable only by the written revealed will of God, a test of truth, which all the parties will allow."[22]

Why go into all this detail to clear the way? It is to whittle away distractions, so the question can be clearly asked and answered using only proper and universally admissible evidence. If Christians are to tolerate doctrinal differences within the same fellowship, there must be a mutual confidence that those who differ are submitting in good faith to a common authority.

From here, Robinson clearly states his position in favor of mixed communion, not just admitting non-immersed Christians to the Table, but also into church membership if they desire. He reasons:

> That it is just and right and agreeable to the revealed will of Christ, that Baptist churches should admit into their fellowship such persons as desire admission on profession of faith and repentance: although they refuse to be baptized by immersion, because they sincerely believe they have been rightly baptized by sprinkling in their infancy.[23]

20 Robinson, *The General Doctrine of Toleration*, 14.
21 Robinson, *The General Doctrine of Toleration*, 15.
22 Robinson, *The General Doctrine of Toleration*, 15–16.
23 Robinson, *The General Doctrine of Toleration*, 16.

Because of indwelling sin and human weakness, few would deny that toleration is necessary in the church. But the crux of the issue is whether such toleration can extend to differences in baptismal views within one congregation. For Robinson, a church is rightly constituted on the issue of baptism if they show toleration for both views.

To support his case, he makes two arguments, one based on "the general principles of analogy" and the other on "the express laws of Jesus Christ."[24] In his first argument, his point is that there is an analogous relationship between the church and the world. Just as nature presents various obstacles and difficulties for human agricultural production, so in the church there are obstacles and difficulties. In natural work, when one encounters an obstacle, if it is not able to be resolved completely, it is best to diminish the difficulty as much as possible, and then get along with the rest of the work in a modified way. Similarly, if a Christian finds it difficult to accept the teaching of believer's baptism, it is in the church's interest to diminish the difficulty of the disagreement by admitting him anyway, since it is a lesser evil "for an unbaptized believer to be incorporated into the church than to lie exposed in the world."[25] In this way, churches can get along with the work of the gospel. After all, since all people deal with various imperfections in doctrine and practice, it is fitting that the church should receive those "imperfect" on the doctrine of baptism, "that they should be permitted to perform all they do know; and patiently borne with till they are able to make further progress."[26]

In another analogical argument, Robinson takes it as a generally agreeable rule that all people should seek, for themselves and for others, to do the most good. In a similar way, in the church, by denying church fellowship to some, "we deprive the church of many wise and worthy members, who might become extremely useful, and we deny them the liberty of exercising such abilities as God gave them for the publick edification." Further, because the primary "visible distinction" of the Christian community ought to be between the regenerate and unregenerate, not between brothers and sisters, Robinson says it is contrary to the constitution of the church and dishonoring to the character of a brother to exclude him from fellowship.[27] In receiving him, the church promotes the good of the individual and the congregation.

Then, from "express laws of Jesus Christ," Robinson highlights several rules with a cumulative force that is quite strong. First, he mentions a law of

---

24 Robinson, *The General Doctrine of Toleration*, 17, 22.
25 Robinson, *The General Doctrine of Toleration*, 19.
26 Robinson, *The General Doctrine of Toleration*, 21.
27 Robinson, *The General Doctrine of Toleration*, 20.

exclusion, which centers on the scriptural lists of vices which merit exclusion from the church, and he notes that none of those lists mention a refusal of believer's baptism. He also mentions laws of toleration, the law of baptism, a law for the exercise of gifts, a law of constitution, and the law of release and deprivation.[28] Under each of these laws, he makes several sub-arguments, though I will not rehash all of them.

In the section on the "law of toleration," Robinson gets to the heart of his hermeneutic of religious toleration, both inside and outside the church:

> This law is, that all christians should enjoy unmolested in the Christian church the right of private judgment. In a multitude of passages in the new testament, the disciples of Christ are exhorted to judge for themselves in all matters of religion and conscience, and this right of self-determination is vindicated not only against magistrates, philosophers and Rabbies, but against fellow-members, as in the xivth of Romans, and even against inspired apostles, as in the 8th and 10th verses of the xxiiid of Matthew. By this law we are bound to allow an universal toleration in all matters, that do not destroy the essence of gospel worship.[29]

Now this is an extraordinary argument, and one that deserves careful examination. Part of Robinson's argument is that in Baptist churches, there is, "strictly speaking, no such thing as publick faith" in the sense of authoritative documents on par with Holy Scripture. Just as each Baptist church has an autonomy of governance, each Christian possesses an autonomy of biblical and theological interpretation which must not be violated. Uniformity is not possible nor expected: "Whatever we publish beside are the private sentiments of different men, and different communities; and it is questionable whether any two churches so exactly agree as bona fide to constitute an uniformity."[30] This basic presupposition of a "right of private judgment" requires mutual toleration within a group and an allowance for a kind of individualism of belief and practice. If there is such latitude from church to church, which all Dissenters affirm, it ought to follow that similar latitude would be allowed among the members of a single church. There is a "natural right" to assemble as churches which the state must acknowledge; and, by analogy, there is a "spiritual right" for the unbaptized to assemble with baptized churches which churches should acknowledge.[31]

---

28 Robinson, *The General Doctrine of Toleration*, 41.
29 Robinson, *The General Doctrine of Toleration*, 23.
30 Robinson, *The General Doctrine of Toleration*, 24.
31 Robinson, *The General Doctrine of Toleration*, 24.

But should not a line be drawn somewhere? He writes that "Toleration ought to extend as far as is consistent with purity of faith and order, and of this each church ought to judge for itself."[32] In other words, each local congregation has authority to determine what kinds of doctrinal and practical latitude it will allow, and Robinson's treatise intends to persuade Baptist churches to broaden to include those sprinkled in infancy. Robinson presents a kind of "theological triage," distinguishing between "errors of faith" and "irregularities of practice."[33] Errors of faith include two categories: (1) a rejection of "the facts recorded in scripture, such as the birth, life, miracles, death, resurrection, ascension, second coming, judgment, and universal dominion of Christ," and (2) "reasonings upon the facts." The latter category is the proper object of ecclesial toleration, not the former. To deny the facts, primary doctrines, makes one a non-Christian with no claim to the Table. However, one who believes the facts, but "reasons obliquely upon them," is a Christian and should be welcomed into fellowship. To give an example, all Christians must reverence Christ's work on the cross ("the fact") and to deny the crucifixion is to be "outside," however, Christians may differ on the nature or extent of the atonement ("reasonings upon the facts") and together remain "inside."

Also to be tolerated, in Robinson's presentation, are "irregularities of practice." Since Christian obedience involves submission to both moral and positive precepts, churches should tolerate irregularities in moral obedience that arise due to infirmity caused by indwelling sin, and churches should tolerate irregularities in positive obedience that arise due to "innocent mental error."[34] For example, the controversy surrounding hymn-singing versus exclusive psalmody in the seventeenth century exposed differences in practice that proved to be more heated and divisive than was necessary, or so Robinson might say. In the end, Robinson argues that unless one knowingly denies a primary doctrine of the faith, he should be tolerated as a member with full privileges in any Baptist church, since any other error does not necessarily destroy the essence or purity of gospel worship.

Next, Robinson notes that "there is...no moral turpitude in mental errors, and the toleration of them is perfectly consistent with the safety of the church, the purity of the faith, and the order of divine worship." In the case of a believer who claims to have been baptized in his infancy,

---

32 Robinson, *The General Doctrine of Toleration*, 24–25.
33 For the term theological triage, see Albert Mohler, "A Call for Theological Triage and Christian Maturity," published July 12, 2005, https://albertmohler.com/2005/07/12/a-call-for-theological-triage-and-christian-maturity.
34 Robinson, *The General Doctrine of Toleration*, 25.

"it is a case of innocent irregularity in obeying a positive institute, and he ought to be allowed to judge for himself."[35] Robinson admits that they are correct who say that baptism is the immersion of a professing believer, and he admits that baptism is a requirement before admission to the Lord's Supper. Nevertheless, Robinson defends that "When people reason thus for themselves they reason rightly: but when they reason thus for another person they claim a right of judgment for him, and consequently deny him that liberty of self judging." In other words, the church has "no authority to deprive him of the right of private judgment."[36]

What if some may reply, "We allow everyone the right to private judgment, but if someone disagrees with our church, they are free to join with another church that is more likeminded"? This is unacceptable to Robinson, who says, "You are required to allow the exercise of private judgment in your own community, not out of it, where your allowance or disallowance operate nothing."[37]

But Robinson is chafing against a longstanding argument in Baptist theology, that baptism is "an initiating ordinance" in the church. Thus, he must revise this understanding of baptism, which leads him to be unwilling to call baptism "an initiating ordinance," stating that he is cautious "not to make more of it than the institutor made."[38] Rather than being an initiating ordinance into the church, baptism is "a publick profession of christianity in general, and that [is] all." He even goes so far as to say, "We affirm, then, that baptism is not a church ordinance, that it is not naturally, necessarily, and actually connected with church fellowship, and consequently that the doctrine of initiating into the christian church by baptism is a confused association of ideas, derived from masters, whose disciples it is no honor to be."[39] These are extraordinary words from one who claims to be a convictional Baptist! Later, he will say "that baptism strictly speaking is neither repentance towards God, nor faith in our Lord Jesus Christ, it is only a profession of these graces, and church fellowship seems in the very nature of the thing to be connected with the graces, and neither with this, nor with any other peculiar mode of professing them."[40]

Finally, Robinson writes that moral duties (like church fellowship) are "of natural and immutable obligation," whereas positive precepts (like

---

35 Robinson, *The General Doctrine of Toleration*, 28.
36 Robinson, *The General Doctrine of Toleration*, 28.
37 Robinson, *The General Doctrine of Toleration*, 28.
38 Robinson, *The General Doctrine of Toleration*, 29.
39 Robinson, *The General Doctrine of Toleration*, 30-31.
40 Robinson, *The General Doctrine of Toleration*, 37.

believer's baptism by immersion) are direct commands in Scripture to be obeyed. Wherever there is some conflict in interpretation among Christians, the moral duty is to take priority over the positive precept. The clear and universal cannot be violated by the less clear and situational. And so, in the case of this conflict over baptism, a genuine Christian is hindered from moral obedience because of a church's restrictive interpretation of a positive precept. This Robinson finds intolerable.

1.4 Robinson's Conclusion

Robinson is eager to assert the difference between civil and ecclesial toleration, and he reassures his interlocutors that they can all join the same cause in defending broad religious toleration in the state, though he desires the same toleration within congregations.[41] He is sympathetic to those who hold the strict communion position, because they view themselves as "the only defenders of this part of the primitive religion," and given how misrepresented and sometimes persecuted Baptists were, no one should be surprised by their tenacity in holding the doctrine strictly.[42] "It is an excess: but it is an excess of virtue, and excessive virtue is the most pardonable of all vices."[43]

Nevertheless, Robinson leverages an emotional appeal as a final argument in favor of a broad toleration of practices within the same congregation. He imagines "a venerable, gray headed old gentleman" entering a strict church meeting, approaching the pastor, and requesting the admission to membership of five men and five women, who are presently waiting in the adjacent room. The old man acknowledges that the petitioners are different from the majority, but they "were well known to have undoubted piety and unspotted morality."

> They held, indeed, infant sprinkling for christian baptism, however, that was no obstacle to him, and he proposed them as members fit to be tolerated in a new testament church, their names were John Calvin, the reformer, William Tindall, the translator of the bible, John Owen, vice chancellor of the learned university of Oxford, Matthew Henry, the expositor, and Isaac Watts, the composer of the psalms and hymns on the table. The ladies were Thecla the writer of the Alexandrian manuscript, Mary, Countess Dowager of Warwick, Lady Mary

---

41 Robinson, *The General Doctrine of Toleration*, 41.
42 Robinson, *The General Doctrine of Toleration*, 43.
43 Robinson, *The General Doctrine of Toleration*, 44.

Vere, Lady Mary Armyne, and Mrs Margaret Baxter, whose praises were in all the churches..."[44]

At this, the old, gray-haired man sits down. Robinson imagines that a long silence follows as "the feelings of the heart rebel against opinion." He imagines tears beginning to flow down the faces of the church members as they consider the Christian service of these men and women. "And you... Pastor of the church...you who are both a guide of the blind, and a teacher of babes...what will you do?"[45] Quite powerful! Robinson's final word is that it lies within the power of the church, led by the pastor, to make such decisions. Ultimately, the church should embrace the liberty granted to her by Jesus Christ, guarding her purity and tolerating misunderstandings, knowing that our hope requires "a patient waiting for Christ, who, when he cometh, will tell us all things!"[46]

2. Contemporary Application

A first point of relevance for our contemporary situation is the mere fact that Robinson engaged in both church and civil discussions which pertained to the extent of liberty. His instincts and tactics for ecclesial toleration stemmed from his fundamental belief in a right to private judgment. This informed his political activism as well, and he often received criticism for his being "too political."[47] There is likely validity to that charge, but Smith notes that "Robinson insisted that obedience to power ordained by God was not blind obedience to human authority. Obedience to government was never at the price of freedom of conscience. When civil government interfered with the right of conscience, Robinson believed that individuals must openly resist it."[48] This led Robinson, and many Dissenters like him, to support the revolutions in the American colonies and in France (though often decrying the bloodshed). Robinson's writing on these topics eventually earned a public rebuke from Edmund Burke. Nevertheless, Robinson was not shy to address government overreach or ecclesial sectarianism in his preaching or writing. For him, this was simply part of the basic Christian life and ministry.

Second, consider the manner in which Robinson engaged in these contentious dialogues. He is a winsome polemicist, and we would do well

---

44 Robinson, *The General Doctrine of Toleration*, 46–47.
45 Robinson, *The General Doctrine of Toleration*, 47.
46 Robinson, *The General Doctrine of Toleration*, 50.
47 Smith, "The Liberty Not to Be a Christian," 156.
48 Smith, "The Liberty Not to Be a Christian," 157.

to learn from his irenic disposition. He expresses his own position with skill and tact, but always with a willingness to see the best of his opponents' motivations. At one point he states that his stricter brothers' refusal "does not proceed from wilful ignorance, obstinacy, spirit of party, bigotry, or any other illiberal disposition: but from a fear of offending God by acting without a sufficient warrant from his written word, the rule of all religious conduct."[49] In another place, he says of those who fail to see believer's baptism by immersion:

> His imperfection is innocent, because he hath exercised all the ability and virtue he has, and his ignorance is involuntary...To deny church-fellowship to persons of genuine virtue, and of, it may be, superior virtue too, is to affix a disgrace and inflict a punishment both without an offence, and in violation of a right. This is a case of involuntary error and there is, there can be no moral turpitude in it.[50]

Once more, at the end of the treatise, he mentions several of the assumptions of his interlocutors which explain their insistence on the strict view: open communion dishonors the initiatory nature of baptism, it opens the door to rashness in changing church policies and to licentious characters, and it can lead to complacency in doctrine.[51] These are but a few examples of the way Robinson shows himself to remember the humanity of those who disagree—these are sincere brothers and sisters in the faith who are earnestly seeking to do what the Bible says. Would that there were more of such a disposition in our contemporary theological discussions!

Third, as a man of the Enlightenment, Robinson was eager to defend and proclaim the rights of the individual. His hermeneutical prioritization of the right to private judgment was no accident. Coercion of belief and practice by the established church led to the bitter persecution of the Baptists prior to the Act of Toleration in 1689, with effects lingering well into the eighteenth century. Thus, Robinson's emphasis on such liberty of conscience is in lockstep with the Baptist tradition. But perhaps he went too far in extending certain implications of private judgment such that he operated with a "lowest common denominator" view of the church's gathered worship. Where is the proper place to draw the line of fellowship? Who gets to decide? Baptists continue to wrestle with the same tensions and questions today.

Related to these concerns, a final point of relevance for contemporary Baptist life is the noticeable absence of a creed or confession of faith in

---

49 Robinson, *The General Doctrine of Toleration*, 10.
50 Robinson, *The General Doctrine of Toleration*, 19–20.
51 Robinson, *The General Doctrine of Toleration*, 37.

Robinson's treatise. This is par for the course at this point in his ministry, and his resistance to creedalism was driven by his prioritization of the right to private judgment. At his church, "he spoke out sharply against the idea that a creedal test should be imposed on persons or churches who applied for help from the Particular Baptist Fund," a fund designated for the ministerial training of Particular Baptist pastors only. In 1776, he published a work defending the deity of Christ, but "refused to begin with the Athanasian Creed."[52] Colin McGahey writes that Robinson's "discomfort with theological systems...stemmed from his high view of individual conscience" and private judgment.[53] Further, in 1789, Robinson wrote a letter, concerning a situation in which a retired minister requested aid from a Baptist organization. Apparently, the terms for receiving retirement income from the board included continual affirmation of a statement of faith. Robinson was outraged and wrote: "They had made a law not to relieve any except they subscribed a creed, a human creed which they sent him; and the first article of which is 'There are three divine persons in the unity of the Godhead!' Absolute nonsense, [awful impiety!] supported by tyranny over men's consciences."[54] This is a startling perspective, which put Robinson out of step with many of his Baptist forebears and colleagues and exposed him to significant theological danger—danger he did not avoid.

3. A Word of Warning

While there is much wisdom to be gleaned from the works of Robert Robinson, his is a cautionary tale. Later in his life he seems to have departed from orthodoxy for Unitarianism.[55] William Cathcart records, "The later

---

52 McGahey, "Transcriber's Preface," 218. In Robinson's work, he writes, "First. We give up Saint Athanasius. He was, we think, no saint: but an enormous sinner. That creed, which is commonly called his, we do not understand; nor can we conceive how the repetition of it can be thought an act of divine worship acceptable to an almighty God; and its damnatory clauses we utterly abhor." (Robert Robinson, *A Plea for the Divinity of Our Lord: In a Pastoral Letter Addressed to a Congregation of Protestant Dissenters, at Cambridge* [Cambridge: Fletcher and Hodson, 1776], 5).
53 McGahey, "Transcriber's Preface," 218.
54 Cited as "Letter from Robinson to Mary Hayes, 4 March 1789, as cited in Ivimey, *History of the English Baptists* 4:52" in Smith, "The Liberty Not to Be a Christian," 163.
55 Though there is some debate about the nature of Robinson's theological shifts, the consensus seems to be that he did embrace "the same rationalism that undermined the General Baptists." See McGahey, "Transcriber's Preface," 218; W. T. Whitley, *A Baptist bibliography: being a register of the chief materials for Baptist history, whether in manuscript or in print, preserved in Great Britain, Ireland and the colonies* (London: Kingsgate Press, 1916–22) 1:214. Also, William Robinson (not related) wrote that Robert Robinson was "one of the most decided Unitarians of the age." (William Robinson, *Select Works of the Rev. Robert Robinson of Cambridge* [London: Heaton & Son, 1861], lxxvii). For a brief assessment of how Robinson was portrayed in these early biographical works, see L. G. Champion, "Robert Robinson, A Pastor in Cambridge" *The Baptist Quarterly 31:5* (1986), 241.

period of Robinson's life was clouded not only by private sorrows, but by his aberration from orthodoxy, and the consequent withdrawal from him of many attached friends and brother ministers. His enthusiastic devotion to liberty, civil and ecclesiastical, attracted to him many persons of skeptical opinions, whose influence was injurious to his spiritual health...." Two such specious associates were none other than the Socinian Joseph Priestly (1733–1804) and the Unitarian Theophilus Lindsey (1723–1808).

We remember Robinson for his famous hymn, "Come Thou Fount of Every Blessing," but by the end of his life he acknowledged that he wished that he could feel as he did when he wrote those words.[56] The sad conclusion is that, at the end of his life, very likely the only lyric he could still sing is, "Prone to wander, Lord, I feel it, prone to leave the God I love." Consistent with this image, one of his biographers, William Robinson, writes in 1861 that "he was like a noble vessel broken from its moorings and drifting out to sea amidst fogs and rocks without a compass or a rudder."[57]

It would be a mistake to dismiss Robinson's arguments because of the state of his theology as his life concluded. It may well be that his views of liberty, conscience, and private judgment *did* set him on a a path that enabled him to break from the moorings of sound doctrine. But even so, should not this sad end prompt our more careful consideration of his arguments and applications? For Robinson, notions of liberty became an obsession, so much so that his liberty could not abide even the blessed bonds of orthodoxy as a slave of the Lord Jesus Christ.

56　William Cathcart, *The Baptist Encyclopaedia: A Dictionary of the Doctrines, Ordinances, Usages, Confessions of Faith, Sufferings, Labors, and Successes, and of the General History of the Baptist Denomination in All Lands : With Numerous Biographical Sketches of Distinguished American and Foreign Baptists, and a Supplement*, vol. 3 (Paris, AR: Baptist Standard Bearer, 1881), 998.
57　Robinson, *Select Works of the Rev. Robert Robinson*, lxxvii.

An Exposition of the Doctrine of Christian Liberty as found in Chapter 21 of the Second London Confession of Faith

James M. Renihan, PhD[1]

1. Of Christian Liberty and Liberty of Conscience

In 1663, the fervently royalist satirist Samuel Butler published a small pamphlet titled *A Proposal Humbly Offered for the Farming of Liberty of Conscience*.[2] With razor sharp sarcasm and acerbic wit, Butler ironically proposed the formation of a select committee of Presbyterian, Congregational and Baptist ministers, including Thomas Manton, John Owen, Thomas Goodwin, John Tombes, William Kiffen and Henry Jessey, who would be charged with the responsibility of selling (farming) certificates of liberty of conscience to various dissenters.

> That the said Grand Commissioners and Farmers of Liberty of Conscience, may have power to constitute under the Publick Seal of the said Office, a convenient number of Spiritual Gagers, who may have and exercise all such Powers, Priviledges, and Authorities, as the Gagers for Excise of Beer and Ale, have, or ought to have and enjoy, and may at any time, in case of Suspition, enter into any house or place, publick or private, to Gage and try the Spirits and Affections of any person or persons; And by Praying, Preaching, or other good Exhortation, disswade from Episcopacy, and the Common-

---

1   This article is largely an excerpt from *Baptist Symbolics, Volume II: To the Judicious and Impartial Reader, A Contextual-Historical Exposition of the Second London Baptist Confession of Faith* (Cape Coral, FL: Founders Ministries, 2022). James M. Renihan is President and Professor of Historical Theology at International Reformed Baptist Seminary, Mansfield, TX.
2   [Samuel Butler], *A Proposal Humbly Offered for the Farming of Liberty of Conscience* (Printed in the Year 1663). The year is notable in that it follows immediately after the Act of Uniformity of late August 1662, a statute which forced puritan ministers out of the Church of England. Butler's *A Proposal Humbly Offered may be accessed in Posthumous Works in Prose and Verse written in the Time of the Civil Wars and the Reign of K. Charles II by Mr. Samuel Butler* (London: Sam. Briscoe, 1715), 58–80. Butler is most famous for his anti-puritan satire Hudibras. See John William Cousin, *A Short Biographical Dictionary of English Literature* (London: J.M. Dent, 1910), 66. Orthography in primary source quotations has been kept as in the original.

Prayer, the better to fit and prepare them to compound for Liberty of Conscience.[3]

These certificates would be purchased for a variety of actions focused on church officers and practices in worship. Mockingly, Butler lays the blame for the civil wars of the 1640s at the feet of these men, naming their pleas for liberty of conscience as the basis for the troubles of the past two decades. Putting words into their mouths, he writes:

> Since nothing can be dearer unto poor Christians than Liberty, or the free exercise of their Judgements and Conscience, which hath kindled that fire in the bowels of the three Kingdoms, which all the precious blood that hath been shed, during those late Troubles, hath not been able totally to extinguish: And since many of us, whose names are affixed, were so profitable instrumental in those late Combustions, as appears all along in our Sermons before the Honourable House of Parliament, in the Years 1642. 43.44.45.46. in exciting the good people of this Nation, to seek and maintain their Christian Liberty, against all Prelaticall and Antichristian Imposition whatsoever....[4]

While Butler's pamphlet is nothing but ridicule, it serves a useful purpose, for it demonstrates the central importance of the doctrine of Christian liberty in the thinking of seventeenth century puritans.

It may be difficult for us to understand just how significant chapter 21 is, both in terms of the Confession itself, and of the theology expressed in the Confession. From our vantage point, well over 300 years from its first writing, we see it as one among many of the doctrines of the Confession. Since it is incorporated, it must be of consequence. But it doesn't get our attention as do chapters 1, 7, 8, 26 etc. To adopt this approach is to underestimate the monumental weight attached to this idea by the reformers and their successors. Consider some of their statements. In his Institutes of the Christian Religion, John Calvin said:

> Now we must entreat of Christian Libertie: the declaration whereof hee must not omit, whose purpose is to comprehend in an abridgement the summe of the doctrine of the Gospel. For it is a thing principally necessarie, and without the knowledge whereof consciences dare in a manner enterprise nothing without doubting, they stumble and start backe in many things, they alway stagger and tremble: but especially it is an appendant of justification, and availaeth not a little to the understanding of the strength thereof.... unlesse that bee fast holden, neither Christ, nor the truth of the Gospell, nor the inward peace of the soule is rightly knowne: Rather

---

3 Butler, *A Proposal Humbly Offered*, 11.
4 Butler, *A Proposal Humbly Offered*, unnumbered page 3.

we must endevour that so necessarie a part of doctrine be not suppressed....[5]

Looking back to the beginning of the Reformation, John Owen asserted:

> The second Principle of the Reformation, whereon the Reformers justified their Separation from the Church of Rome, was this, That Christian People were not tyed up unto blind Obedience unto Church Guides, but were not only at Liberty, but also obliged to judge for themselves, as unto all things that they were to believe and practise in Religion and the Worship of God. They knew that the whole Fabrick of the Papacy did stand on this Basis or Dunghil, that the Mistery of Iniquity was cemented by this Device, namely, that the People were ignorant, and to be kept in Ignorance, being obliged in all things unto an implicite Obedience unto their pretended Guides. And that they might not be capable of, nor fit for any other condition, they took from them the only means of their Instruction unto their Duty, and the Knowledge of it, that is, the Use of the Holy Scripture. But the first Reformers did not only vindicate their Right unto the Use of the Scripture itself, but insisted on it as a Principle of the Reformation, (and without which they could never have carried on their Work) that they were in all concernments of Religion to judge for themselves.[6]

In his comments on this section of WCF, David Dickson wrote:[7]

> Well then, do not the Papists err, who contradict this, both in doctrine (because they teach that the pope of Rome, and bishops in their own diocesses, may, by their own authority, praeter Scripturam, besides the word make laws which oblige and bind the conscience, under the pain of everlasting death); and in practice, (because they have obtruded, and do obtrude many ecclesiastical rites and ceremonies, as necessary in worship, without any foundation in Scripture?)[8]

Finally, Samuel Bolton penned:

> There are two great things Christ hath intrusted into the hands of his Church: First, Christian faith. Secondly, Christian liberty. And as we are to contend earnestly for the maintenance of the faith, as the Apostle saith, Iude 3. So also for the maintenance of Christian libertie, against all oppugners and underminers of it. Gal. 5.1. Stand fast in the libertie wherewith Christ made you free. And much like to this is that of the Apostle, You are

---

5   John Calvin, *The Institution of Christian Religion*, Trans. Thomas Norton (London: Ioyce Norton and R. Whitaker: 2017), 403. Calvin's treatment is exceedingly helpful.

6   John Owen, *An Enquiry Into the Original, Nature, Institution, Power, Order and Communion of Evangelical Churches* (London: Nath. Ponder, 1681), 294.

7   The following abbreviations are used: Westminster Confession of Faith, WCF; Savoy Declaration, Savoy; Second London Confession of Faith, 2LCF.

8   David Dickson, *Truths Victory Over Error* (Edinburgh: John Reed, 1684), 152.

bought with a price, be no more the servants of men, 1 Cor. 7.23.[9]

These quotations make the point very well. The doctrine of Christian Liberty is central to our understanding of the Christian life. As Calvin says, it has a direct relationship to justification. As soon as we submit to human laws in religion, we lose our freedom in Christ. He alone has a right to command what he wills, and no one may add to his commands. We could go so far as to say that this doctrine is placed here to serve as the head of the next major section of the Confession. The order is not accidental. From chapter 21 to chapter 30, every doctrine is affected by the theology of Christian liberty—some more than others—some more overtly and directly—but nonetheless all are impacted. That may seem like an undocumented sweeping statement but consider these points.

The next chapter, 22, *Of Worship and the Sabbath Day* contemplates the nature and obligations of worship and the Lord's Day, especially in relation to the regulative principle of worship. The point of this tenet is that its neglect is an infringement of liberty and the expression of tyranny over the conscience. Chapter 23, *Of Lawful Oaths and Vows* carries forward the theme. The language of 23.1 ties these matters together when it states *A lawful oath is a part of religious worship.* Chapter 24, *Of the Civil Magistrate* addresses an important question. Must believers obey those political rulers? and answers positively, teaching that when they function in their divinely appointed roles we honor the Fifth Commandment by our submission. Chapter 25, *Of Marriage* describes the Scriptural laws about marriage. Are there any restraints on Christian freedom in relation to marriage?

Chapter 26 through 30 speak about ecclesiology and could legitimately be considered a separate unit. But in some ways, they continue the theme of Christian liberty and may be considered a subset. In Chapter 26, the foundational idea is that Christ is Lord of the church and no one may intrude on his lordship, for he expresses his rule in very specific ways. In Chapter 27, *Of the Communion of the Saints*, his headship raises an important question, namely, what are the obligations of saints to one another? Chapter 28, *Of Baptism and the Lord's Supper* are framed in such a way as to emphasize Christ's lordship and the believer's obligation to him. Chapter 29 and 30, *Of Baptism and Of the Lord's Supper* simply provide further detail.

In each of these cases, the Confession sets out a framework by which Christians may understand what Christ commands, so that they may be wary

---

9   Samuel Bolton, *The True Bounds of Christian Freedom* (London: Austin Rice, 1656), 8-9.

of the inventions, intrusions and legalisms of men. All these doctrines were, in the Seventeenth century, subject to *religious* abuse. Their purity needed to be expressed in confessional terms. As a result this doctrine takes on great importance.

1.1 Christian Liberty Defined

1. The Liberty which Christ hath purchased for Believers under the Gospel, consists in their freedom from the guilt of Sin, the condemning wrath of God, the Rigour and (a) Curse of the Law; and in their being delivered from this present evil (b) World, Bondage to (c) Satan, and Dominion (d) of Sin; from the (e) Evil of Afflictions; the Fear, and Sting (f) of Death, the Victory of the Grave, and (g) Everlasting Damnation; as also in their (h) free access to God; and their yielding Obedience unto him not out of a slavish fear, (i) but a Child-like love, and willing mind.

All which were common also to Believers under the Law (k) for the substance of them; but under the new Testament, the Liberty of Christians is further enlarged in their freedom from the yoke of the Ceremonial Law, to which the Jewish Church was subjected; and in greater boldness of access to the Throne of Grace; and in fuller Communications of the (l) Free Spirit of God, then Believers under the Law did ordinarily partake of.

a Gal. 3.13.

b Gal. 1.4.

c Act. 26.18.

d Rom. 8.3.

e Rom. 8.28.

f 1 Cor. 15.54,55,56.57.

g 2 Thes. 1.10.

h Rom. 8.15.

i Luk. 1.74,75. 1 Joh. 4 18.

k Gal. 3,9:14.

l Joh. 7.38,39. Heb. 10, 19,20,21.

As noted in the quotation from Calvin, Christian doctrine takes seriously the relationship between Christ's death and the believer's liberty. Freedom is not simply granted, it is purchased—it came at a price, and the payment is the death of the Son of God. The language is quite powerful. The Confession asserts that Christ has purchased liberty for believers. It was an intentional accomplishment of his sacrifice, related to justification, adoption, sanctification, assurance, the Law of God, worship and the church. Christ, by his death, delivered his people from sin and its many consequences, and set them free for many blessings, all of which must be resolved back to the death of Christ.

This freedom consists of deliverances. Christ's purchase of liberty removes from us (or removes us from) a series ten effects of sin, divided into four sections. They are expressed in the Confession as things that were against us. This extensive list is full of wonderful truth. Believers are freed from (1) *the guilt of sin* (cf. 6.2 and 3). This is the real guilt before God to which they were subject, and it is removed. (2) They are freed from *the condemning wrath of God*. While this is the only occurrence of this phrase in the Confession, its meaning is not obscure (cf. 3.3, 6.3 and 32.2). (3) Thirdly, they are free from the rigor and curse of the Law (7.2, 19.6) which required *personal entire exact and perpetual obedience* (19.1), demands no one could fulfill after Adam's fall (6.1–4, 9.3, 10.2). William Ames similarly stated the doctrine, "The first fruit of adoption is that Christian liberty. (*sic*) Whereby all believers are set at liberty by a manumission, as it were from the bondage of the Law, sin and the world."[10]

As is common throughout the document, a semi-colon separates ideas, introducing a familiar trio, though ordered slightly differently.[11] Christians are liberated from the world, the devil and the flesh (cf. 1.1, 5.6. 17. 1 and 3). (4) They are freed from the world, modified from Galatians 1.4 *to this present evil world*, that which the *English Annotations* call "this most corrupt state."[12] (5) Deliverance is from *bondage to Satan*, their wicked overlord, and (6) the flesh expressed as the dominion of sin. In each case, the Christian is delivered from the power of the thing named. The world—this evil age—no longer can claim the believer as its dutiful citizen. Satan is no longer master, and the flesh has no dominion.

The third segment of the ten consists of a single phrase, (7) *deliverance from the evil of afflictions*. The language here must be noted carefully. The Confession does not assert that we are delivered from afflictions themselves, but rather from their evil. Based in their understanding of texts such as Genesis 50.20 or Romans 8.28, the confessors recognized that although

---

10 William Ames, *The Marrow of Sacred Divinity* (London: Henry Overton, 1642), 139.
11 The phrase "the world, the flesh and the devil" though popular in this order, is not found in the Bible.
12 *English Annotations on Galatians* 1.4. There is no printer's mark on the page. (Anon.) *Annotations Upon all the Books of the Old and New Testament* (London: John Legatt, 1645).

Christian believers will suffer afflictions, they do so in a manner different from the unbeliever. Thomas Manton is very helpful when he writes:

> Affliction doth not separate from God, 'tis a means to make us draw nigh to him. Poverty, Sickness, Blindness, Loss of Goods, let a Man be never so low and loathsom, yet if in a state of Grace, the Lord taketh pleasure in him, and he is near and dear to God.... The Evil of Affliction, is but for a moment, like Rain, it drieth up of its own accord: But the Evil of Sin is for ever, unless it be pardoned and taken away. Sin is the Cause of all the Evils of Affliction; therefore when we complain, we should complain, not so much of the Smart, as of the Cause of it.[13]

The fourth subsection follows. While separated from the previous phrase by punctuation, the subsequent items are related to what precedes, for the greatest affliction is death. Like a crescendo, the Confession moves from the lesser to the greater. (8) Liberty delivers Christ's disciples from *the fear, and sting of death*. The statement is based on a collation of Hebrews 2.15 and the supplied verses, 1 Corinthians 15.54-57. In his commentary on the Hebrews verse, William Gouge poignantly expressed this doctrine:

> Fear is a disturbed passion, arising from the expectation of some evil which we would shun: For the Greek word cometh from a Verb that signifieth to flee from and this word here used by the Apostle, is sometimes put for flight. Men use to flee from such things as they fear; and if men could, they would flee from and avoid death. Death therefore being taken to be the greatest of evils, and man continually expecting it, must needs fill mans heart with fear, even fear of a bodily death. ... But to such as are instructed in the nature of sin (which addeth a sting to death,) and in the resurrection of the body, and the intolerable and everlasting torment of body and soul in hell, death must needs be a far greater fear, till they have some assurance of their deliverance from it: For death as it was first inflicted for sinne, is the very entrance into eternal damnation; how then can the thought and remembrance of death be but very dreadful?[14]

By his death and resurrection, believers are released from this terrible dread. In their comment on 1 Corinthians 15.55 ("O death, where is thy sting?") the English Annotations exultantly state "This is a song of triumph sung by the Apostle, ravished as it were, by the conquest of death."[15] (9) Victory over the grave follows, joined with (10) victory over everlasting

---

13 Thomas Manton, *A Practical Exposition of the Lord's Prayer* (London: Jonathan Robinson, 1684), 494-497.

14 William Gouge, A *Learned and Very useful Commentary on the Whole Epistle to the Hebrewes* (London: Joshua Kirton, 1655), 126.

15 English Annotations on 1 Corinthians 15.55, sigla FF recto.

damnation. The grave is not the final resting place for believers (31.2), nor will they suffer the consequences of sin (32.2). This is the final victory, the reversal of the curse and all of its effects. Christ has set us free from the worst of miseries—banishment from the presence of God. In place of damnation, we receive eternal life.

Purchased liberty also consists of privileges, for it is not only deliverance from these things, it also brings tremendous benefits. The first is free access to God. John Owen says that "this is the great fundamental privilege of the gospel, that believers, in all their holy worship, have liberty, boldness, and confidence, to enter with it and by it into the gracious presence of God."[16] This is a tremendous blessing. Sinners, the fallen rebellious sons of Adam, have immediate access to the throne room of heaven. This free approach to the Father produces a change in their response to Him, for they no longer obey from slavish fear, the reaction a servant gives to a harsh master. Rather, the work of Christ received by faith gives a new understanding of the love, mercy and kindness of God, so that the believer's service is obedience from a child-like love. Liberty brings joyful compliance to God's will, a devoted response to the gracious acts expressed towards us. We do not obey because we fear condemnation; we obey because we love to please our Father in heaven.

The first article is divided into two sub-paragraphs, the second addressing an important redemptive-historical question previously raised in 8.6 and 11.1. Since these blessings flow from the person and work of Christ, how did Old Testament believers, especially those who lived under the Mosaic law, experience them? This is a reasonable inquiry. In response, we are taught that in substance, all believers have enjoyed this privilege. Though some important distinctions must be noted, in principle, these liberties belong to all believers. Those under the law enjoyed all these things, but not in precisely the same way. They were set free from the guilt of sin, condemning wrath and the other freedoms mentioned. They had true spiritual access to God, for when they prayed God heard their prayers. Nevertheless, our liberty is far greater than theirs. Under the New Testament our liberty is enlarged since we are granted freedom from the ceremonial law. We are not bound to the observance of the stipulations of the Mosaic code to which Old Testament believers (and Christ himself cf. 8.4) were subject. Similarly, now we enjoy greater boldness of access to God's throne, a gloss on Ephesians 3.12. How

---

16   John Owen, *A Continuation of the Exposition ... to the Hebrews* (London: Nathaniel Ponder, 1680) on Hebrews 10.19. The exposition of each chapter has its own pagination. This quotation may be found on page 57 of the exposition of Hebrews 10. The printer's mark at the bottom of the page is *Hhhhh*.

is this? Because our access is through Christ. We are no longer subject to ceremonial uncleanness and must follow prescribed rituals to qualify for worship; when we sin, we need not bring an offering to the priest so that we might be restored. As John Trapp said, "Christ take(s) his people and lead(s) them into his fathers presence."17 A further privilege granted to New Covenant believers is the reception of fuller communications of the Spirit in contrast with that which believers under the Law did ordinarily partake of. Though Old Covenant believers knew the work of the Holy Spirit in some measure, (Deuteronomy 34.9, Psalm 104.30, 139.7, etc.), John 7.37-39 (a proof text for this assertion) indicates that there was a distinct difference between their experience and that of God's people after Pentecost. The final words of the paragraph make this point. The Spirit has been poured out, so that believers now enjoy greater endowments of his power. In their gloss on John's text, the English Annotations point to Joel 2.28 and state "that is, those visible graces ... which flourished after the Ascension of Christ."18

1.2 The Boundaries of Christian Liberty

> 2. God alone is (m) Lord of the Conscience, and hath left it free from the Doctrines and Commandments of men, (n) which are in any thing contrary to his Word, or not contained in it. So that to Believe such Doctrines, or obey such Commands out of Conscience, (o) is to betray true liberty of Conscience; and the requiring of an (p) implicit Faith, and absolute and blind Obedience, is to destroy Liberty of Conscience, and Reason also.
>
> m Jam. 4.12, Rom. 14.4.
>
> n Act. 4.19 & 5.29. 1 Cor. 7.23. Mat. 15.9:
>
> o Col: 2.20 22,23:
>
> p 1 Cor. 3.5: 2 Cor. 1.24.

The second paragraph contains one of the most famous statements on Christian Liberty ever written. It deserves to be memorized and repeated over and over so that we might understand the sweeping nature of its assertion. It begins with a claim to unique right and authority. *God alone is Lord of the Conscience*, an extension of the fact that *God alone is Lord*. This universal statement is extended to express the explicit divine declaration that he only is the judge of morality. No one may intrude on his domain.

---

17   John Trapp, *A Commentary or Exposition upon all the Books of the New Testament* (London: Nath. Ekins, 1656), 761.
18   *English Annotations,* on John 7.39 sigla I verso.

The first place to look in the discussion of liberty of conscience is to God. In this case, conscience is the sphere of his lordship. Using similar language, William Perkins defines *conscience*:

> Conscience is a knowledge ioyned with a knowledge. For by conscience we knowe what we know; and by it we knowe that thing of our selues which God knoweth of vs. The naturall condition of euery mans conscience is this; that it is placed in the middle betweene man and God, vnder God and aboue man. And this naturall condition hath two parts: the one is the subiection of conscience to God and his word; the second is a power whereby the conscience is ouer the man to vrge and binde him. Of the first, we haue this rule, that God alone by his word doeth onely binde conscience properly: for he is the onely Lord of the conscience, which created it, and gouerns it. He againe is the onely lawe-giuer, that hath power to saue or destroy the soule, for the keeping and breaking of his Lawes. Iam. 4. 12. Againe, mans conscience is knowne to none but to God, and it is he onely that giues libertie to the conscience, in regard of his owne lawes. Vpon this it followeth, that no mans commandement or Lawe can of it selfe, and by it owne soueraigne power binde conscience, but doeth it onely by the authoritie and vertue of the written word of God, or some part thereof.[19]

Perkins precisely expresses the intent of the shared statement of WCF, Savoy and 2LCF.

Since God alone is Lord, the conscience is free from the religious dictates of men. This is expressed in two ways. The conscience is free *from the doctrines of men* and from the *commandments of men* which are *contrary to his word, or not contained in it*. These phrases indicate that the doctrine of Christian liberty relates to religious matters. It is not a door to libertinism, as if Christians are not bound to obedience to humans in some senses. The following chapters, especially 24 and 25 make this clear. In matters of faith, however, God claims exclusive right. If a commandment requires thoughts or actions that contravene the Word of God, or extend beyond its boundaries, there is no religious obligation in it.

Contending that the Pope and Bishops have no right to impose religious acts on people, David Dickson expresses the common doctrine of the reformed churches as he "confutes" their ideas:

> By what reasons are they confuted?
>
> (1) Because, there is one Law-giver, who is able to save, and to destroy; Iames 4. 12. Therefore no Pope, no Prelate, nor any meer man, can be a Law-giver. (2) Because, Christ rejects the

---

19 William Perkins, *The First Part of the Cases of Conscience* (Cambridge: John Legat, 1604), 43.

Commandments of men, from the worship of God; Matth. 15. 9. (3) Because, the Apostles refused, to obey the orders of the Council, since they were contrary to the Commands of God; Acts 4. 19. Acts 5. 29. (4) because, the Lord threatens to do a marvellous work among his people, because they drew near to him with theirmouth (as the most part of the Ceremonial service, is but a drawing near to God with the mouth,) but had their hearts removed far from him; Isaiah 29. 13, 14. (5) Because, Christ expresly forbids such subjection and obedience to the Commands of men; Matth. 23. 9, 10. 1 Cor. 7. 23. (6) because, the Apostles themselves forbids (sic) all will-worship, such as the Popish Ceremonies are; Col. 2. 18, 21, 22, 23. (8) Because, the Apostle Paul, withstood these false Brethren, unawars brought in, who came in privily, to spie out his liberty, which he had in Christ Jesus, that they might bring him into bondage, to whom he gave place by subjection, no not for an hour; that the truth of the Gospel, might continue: where he lays so much weight upon Christian liberty; that, if that were taken away, the truth of the Gospel, would perish likewise; Gal. 2. 4, 5. (9) Because, the Apostle commands Believers, to stand fast in their liberty, wherewith Christ hath made them free, and not to be intangled again with the yoke of bondage; Gal. 5. 1. (10) Because Ceremonies are superstitious, being a vice opposite to Religion in the excess, commanding more in the Worship of God, than he requires in his Worship.[20]

This rejection of man-made doctrines and practices was central to the worship and practice of the reformed churches, but also, as we have seen in Samuel Butler's mocking words, a matter of principle in puritan thinking. Like 8.9, this argument supports the assertion in 26.4 that the Pope is antichrist. The imposition of human laws dethrones Christ and usurps God's rightful place as *Lord of the conscience*. George Downame wrote:

Herein therefore the Church of Rome is also an enemy to Christian liberty, not only in burthening Christians with an heape of innumerable traditions and ceremonies; but chiefly, in imposing them vpon the conscience: teaching, that the traditions of the Church are with like reuerence, and equall affection of piety to be receiued, as the written word of God; and that the commandements of the Church, euen concerning outward things, doe binde the conscience, And although many of their ceremonies be wicked; more, ridiculous; most of them, superfluous; yet so absurd they are, as to impose them to bee obserued, not only with opinion of necessity, as binding the conscience, but also of worship, of perfecton, of merit, of spirituall efficacy.[21]

Liberty of conscience is destroyed by *believing* human *doctrines* or obeying *human commands out of conscience*, a phrase intended to condemn submission

---

20 David Dickson, *Truths Victory Over Error* (Edinburgh: John Reed, 1684), 152–53.
21 George Downame, *The Christians Freedome* (London: William Webb, 1635), 102–03.

to any doctrine or command not stated or contained in Scripture. To do so is to *betray* the benefits purchased by Christ. The reason for this destruction is that by following human doctrines or commands, we have dethroned God and placed another authority in his stead.

Liberty of conscience is also destroyed by *requiring an implicit faith*.[22] In the confessions, *implicit faith* refers to any doctrine or practice mandated by a religious authority, as if commanded by and pleasing to God, simply on the basis of human authority. Muller defines implicit faith as trust in "'what the church believes' without knowing the objective contents of faith."[23] Dickson parses the phrase well, refuting it with six points: (1) implicit faith and blind obedience require one to do that of which they have not been persuaded is the will of God, (2) "all things must be examined" and proved "by the Rule of the Word;" (3) because Paul tells the Thessalonians to "prove all things;" (4) "Because blind obedience makes us the servants of men ... against the command of Christ;" (5) because "absolute obedience is only due to God;" and (6) "because, every man ought to be ready to render a reason of the hope which is in him" which no one can do based on "implicit faith."[24]

To follow these paths *betrays* and *destroys liberty of conscience* and also *reason*. To *betray* is "treacherous and disloyal," to *destroy* removes true liberty and in its place ensnares in a web of manmade legislation.[25] *Reason* may also be *betrayed* and *destroyed*, for sanctified reason, informed by the Word of God,

---

22 The phrase "implicit faith" may be used in different ways. For example, William Ames uses it approvingly. In part 2 of the *Marrow*, chapter 4 on Faith, he writes:

31. Faith is partly Implicite, and partly Explicite.

32. Implicite Faith is that whereby the truths of Faith are believed, not distinctly in themselves, but in their common principle.

33. That common principle wherein all things to be believed in this manner believed are contained, is not the Church, but the Scripture. Act 24.14. Who believe all things which are written in the Law and in the Prophets.

34. He that believeth that the Scripture is every way true, he doth implicitly believe all things which are contained in the Scriptures, Psa 119.86, compared with Verse 28. 33. All thy precepts are truth itself; open mine eyes, that I may see the wonders of thy Law. Teach me the way of thy statuts, which I will keepe to the end. David did believe that those were wonderful, and to be holily kept, which he did not yet sufficiently understand.

35. This implicite Faith is good and necessary, but it is not of itself sufficient to salvation; neither indeed hath it in it selfe, the true reason of faith, if it subsist by itself: for it cannot be that the will be effectually affected, and embrace that as good, which it doth not at all distinctly know. Rom 20.14. (sic) How shall they believe him of whom they have not heard?

See Ames, *Marrow*, 255-256. In the case of 2LCF21.2 it carries a strictly negative connotation.
23 Richard Muller, *Dictionary of Latin and Greek Theological Terms* (Grand Rapids: Baker, 2017), s.v. fides implicita.
24 Dickson, *TVOE*, 154-155.
25 *Oxford English Dictionary, s.v. betray* 1.a.

will recognize the spiritual devastation following in the wake of submission to human dictates.

1.3 The Perversion of Christian Liberty

> 3. They who upon pretence of Christian Liberty do practice any sin, or cherish any sinfull lust; as they do thereby pervert the main design of the Grace of the Gospel, (q) to their own Destruction; so they wholy destroy (r) the end of Christian Liberty, which is, that being delivered out of the hands of all our Enemies we might serve the Lord without fear in Holiness, and Righteousness before him, all the days of our Life.
>
> q Rom. 6.1,2.
>
> r Gal. 5.13. 2 Pet. 2.18.–21.

David Dickson asserts that the focus of this paragraph is on "libertines" and "antinomians," both of which sought refuge under the general banner of Christianity. He charges the libertines with taking "away all difference, between Good and Evil" and antinomians with "almost the very same tenet." Those who sin under pretense, who use the doctrine of liberty as a means to permit evil, and others who cherish any sinful lust are condemned in the strongest terms. They pervert the main design of the grace of the Gospel which while granting free forgiveness to sinners calls them to a life of obedience to God's commandments (11.2, 16.2, 19.5, 6 and 7). Any who do or teach in the libertine or antinomian manner are guilty of perversion of, not just Christian Liberty, but of the grace of God in the gospel itself. Such instruction is an attack on the very heart of Christianity. It results in two things, (1) personal destruction, since it evidences the fact that this person has failed to understand the Gospel and its implications, exposing him to damnation, and (2) it destroys the end (purpose) *of Christian Liberty*. The goal is twofold, expressed in the words of Zacharias recorded in Luke 1.74, deliverance from the hands of our enemies in order that we might serve the *Lord without fear in holiness and righteousness before him all the days of our lives*. True liberty is not license; it is rather the freedom to live a life unto God, pursuing holiness and righteousness. Those who understand the doctrine do not have to wonder if their acts please him. Based on his revelation, they know what pleases him, and freely pursue it with pleasure. In the continuation of Matthew Poole's annotations, John Collinges penned these fitting words:

> Thus Zacharias by an infallible Spirit, expounds the Covenants, and Oaths of God to Abraham, and David, not as

they appear to us at first view, as if they were promises of a meer temporal Kingdom, and a Victory for the Jews over their Enemies, together with a splendid state for them; which was all the Scribes and Pharisees, and the generality of the Jews expected from the Messiah, but as confirming Gods resolution to send the Jews a Saviour, who should save them from their Sins, the guilt and Dominion of them, and from the Power of Hell, and purchase a spiritual liberty for them to serve the Lord all their days, without fear in holiness, and righteousness, which indeed, was the true end of the Messiahs coming. Thus far now the Song of this holy Man respected Christ, whom he sheweth to be sent from the free Grace, and Mercy of God, yet in performance of Gods truth and faithfulness, according to his Oath, and promises, and to be therefore sent to deliver his People from their Enemies, and to purchase for them a spiritual liberty not to Sin, but to serve the Lord without fear, in Holiness and Righteousness.[26]

2. For Devotion

O Glorious Jesus! behold, to thee we bow, and humbly implore thy blessing, in whom all fulness dwells. Accomplish in us, we pray, those gracious purposes for which thou didst assume the humane Nature, and suffer a painful and ignominious Death. Teach us, O Lord, by thy Word, and thy example, the sole way to that Bliss for which we were created. Give us an assur'd pardon of all our sins, and the priviledge of becoming the Sons of God: Possess us with the joyful hope of an eternal Life, purchas'd for us by our Redeemer's Death. O Almighty Redeemer, destroy in us the works of the Devil: Deliver us (for none else can) from the power of every sin. Set us at liberty to run the wayes of thy Commandments; thy Service is perfect freedom. Give us the special Assistance of thy Grace, that we may wean our Affections from all vain desires, and clear our thoughts from all impertinent fancies, that our lives may be intirely dedicated to thee, and all the Faculties of our Souls to thy holy Service: That our minds may continually study thy Knowledge, and our Wills grow every day stronger in thy Love: Our Memories may faithfully lay up thy Mercy, and both Tongue and Heart be continually disposed, and often employ'd to praise thee; to praise thy incomparable Love, which has done and suffer'd so much for lost Mankind. O let the continual memory of thy bitter Passion and Death, make us despise the Goods or Ills that we meet with here, compar'd to the advancing our selves or others in the esteem of what we hope hereafter; through the Sufferings and Merits of thee our Lord Jesus Christ. Amen.[27]

---

26 *Annotations upon the Holy Bible* (London: Thomas Parkhurst et.al., 1685), Volume II, no pagination; on Luke 1.79. Samuel Palmer, *The Nonconformists Memorial* (London: Button and Son, 1803), III:11 indicates that John Collinges supplied the comments on the four Gospels.
27 (Anon.) *Reform'd Devotions* (London: Joseph Watts, 1687), 292–294.

Thomas Helwys, Roger Williams, and Pre-Enlightenment Arguments for Religious Liberty

Jesse Owens, PhD

It is often assumed that the more a society embraces religious skepticism, the more tolerant it will become of various religions and religious practices. Of course, this would lead one to conclude that the influence of the Enlightenment might have led to greater religious toleration, which was indeed true in some cases in the eighteenth century. However, the underlying premise that religious skepticism leads to greater religious toleration is not necessarily accurate, as John Coffey has ably demonstrated in the political theory of Thomas Hobbes.[1] In *Leviathan*, Hobbes, a radical skeptic for his age, "argued for freedom of internal thought, not for freedom of nonconformist worship or expression."[2] Hobbes did not favor religious toleration for Dissenters. Radical skepticism, for Hobbes, did not necessarily lead to an affirmation of religious toleration.

The earliest defenders of religious toleration in the seventeenth century, in England and America, were "devout believers," not skeptics.[3] Many of these devout believers were Baptists, and a large percentage of them were General Baptists though many Particular Baptists defended religious toleration as well. Writing in the 1610s-1650s, on both sides of the Atlantic, these Baptists were not influenced by the writings of John Locke on toleration, since Locke did not publish on the subject until the end of the seventeenth century.[4]

In a fascinating chapter entitled "The Evangelical Encounter with the Enlightenment," Catherine A. Brekus details early American evangelicals'

---

1   John Coffey, "Scepticism, Dogmatism and Toleration in Seventeenth-Century England," in *Persecution and Pluralism: Calvinist and Religious Minorities in Early Modern Europe 1550-1700*, ed. Richard Bonney and D. J. B. Trim (Bern, Switzerland: Peter Lang, 2006), 155-156
2   Coffey, "Scepticism," 159.
3   Coffey, "Scepticism," 176.
4   English Baptists would include men such as Thomas Helwys, Leonard Busher, John Murton, Edward Barber, Henry Denne, Samuel Fisher, Henry Danvers, and Thomas Collier. In the American context, Roger Williams and John Clarke also advocated for religious toleration. But other Puritans such as John Goodwin and Henry Robinson defended religious toleration as well. These men and their writings are dealt with in more detail in John Coffey, "Puritanism and Liberty Revisited," *The Historical Journal*, 41, no. 4 (1998): 961-985.

relationship with Enlightenment principles. To be sure, evangelicals did not imbibe Enlightenment ideas and ideals wholesale.[5] But they also did not reject the Enlightenment altogether. Brekus maintains that evangelicals were "especially attracted to John Locke's emphasis on firsthand experience as the basis of knowledge," which she sees as underpinning some evangelical's emphasis on "experimental" religion.[6]

Yet Brekus proceeds to argue that evangelical arguments for religious toleration were shaped by Enlightenment philosophy and "the right of the sovereign individual to choose his own government, to pursue his own economic interests in the marketplace, and to worship according to the dictates of his own conscience."[7] Of Samuel Davies (1723-1761), one of the main figures in the chapter, Brekus writes, "His defense of individual religious freedom became a hallmark of the evangelical movement."[8]

It is at this point where I find myself in partial disagreement with Brekus.[9] Her argument seems to overemphasize the role of the Enlightenment on an evangelical understanding of religious toleration and the dictates of conscience. Summarizing the thought of Davies, Brekus writes, "Not even the king had the right to elevate himself over God by acting as the ultimate judge of religious truth."[10] But this line of thought had appeared among English and American Protestants over a century before in the writings of Thomas Helwys and Roger Williams.

To be clear, Helwys and Williams were not the primary influences on those who argued for religious toleration in England or America in the eighteenth century, though Isaac Backus (1724-1806) had clearly read the writings of Roger Williams. However, Helwys's and Williams's arguments for religious toleration preceded Locke's publications on the subject by nearly three-quarters of a century.[11] Thus, Protestant arguments for religious toleration, and one's ability to follow the dictates of conscience in matters of religion, need not necessarily be rooted in Enlightenment philosophy.

---

5   Catherine A. Brekus, "The Evangelical Encounter with the Enlightenment" in *Turning Points in the History of American Evangelicalism*, ed. Heath W. Carter and Laura Rominger Porter (Grand Rapids: Eerdmans, 2017), 31.
6   Brekus, "Evangelical Encounter," 31.
7   Brekus, "Evangelical Encounter," 34.
8   Brekus, "Evangelical Encounter," 36.
9   Brekus is dealing almost exclusively with eighteenth-century American evangelicals. I do not disagree with her premise in its entirety. What I want to emphasize is the way in which arguments for religious toleration in the previous century, even in the American context, were not dependent upon the writings of John Locke.
10   Brekus, "Evangelical Encounter," 35.
11   Milton's *Areopagitica* (1644) did make a case for religious toleration, but not to the extent of Helwys's argument for universal religious toleration.

1. Thomas Helwys (c. 1575–c. 1616)

Helwys's most ardent defense of religious liberty appeared in print in the early 1600s. In *A Short Declaration of the Mystery of Iniquity* (1612), Helwys contends that all people should have religious freedom. And Helwys really meant all. He wrote: "Neither may the King be judged between God and man. Let them be heretics, Turks, Jews, or whatsoever it appertains not to the earthly power to punish them in the least measure."[12] The Act of Toleration (1689) granted religious freedom to Trinitarians but denied religious freedom to anti-Trinitarians and Catholics.

Helwys simply did not believe that civil magistrates should exercise authority in religious matters. Helwys wrote to King James, "The king is a mortal man and not God, therefore he has no power over the immortal souls of his subjects, to make laws and ordinances for them and to set spiritual lords over them. If the king has the authority to make spiritual lords and laws, then he is an immortal God and not a mortal man."[13] This almost certainly landed Helwys in Newgate prison where he died sometime around 1616.

It is important to note that Helwys defended universal religious toleration, not on the basis of Enlightenment principles and ideals. Instead, he based them upon a nuanced interpretation of key biblical passages. He, like many Baptists in the following decades, saw, unlike many of their Protestant (and Puritan) counterparts, discontinuity between Old Testament Israel and Christian nations. This sense of discontinuity underpinned their arguments for religious toleration, not Enlightenment principles.[14] Locke's argument for religious freedom would not appear in print for nearly seventy-five more years, but at the very beginning of the seventeenth century, Helwys was arguing for universal religious toleration. This demonstrates an early Protestant argument for religious liberty that is not in any way based upon the Enlightenment.

2. Roger Williams (1603–1683)

A similar argument could be made for Roger Williams. Williams opposed

---

12 Thomas Helwys, *A Short Declaration of the Mystery of Iniquity* (London: 1612), 69. Spelling modernized.
13 This appears as a handwritten inscription at the beginning of *A Short Declaration of the Mystery of Iniquity.*
14 Coffey makes this case better than any other I have seen in print. See Coffey, "Puritanism and Liberty," 971–977.

the Puritan view of the relationship between the government and the civil magistrate. As James Byrd explains, "Puritans believed that the bible demonstrated that Baptists, Quakers, and other so-called heretics and pagans deserved punishment because they threatened both civil peace and religious orthodoxy in the 'Bible Commonwealths' of New England."[15] Williams was vehemently opposed to such notions. Consequently, he was exiled from the Massachusetts Bay Colony in 1635 but went on to found both the colony of Rhode Island and the first Baptist church in America in Providence, Rhode Island.

Williams's most well-known work on religious liberty was *The Bloudy Tenent* (1644). In this work Williams argued for complete religious toleration over the bloody tenet of religious persecution of heretics. For Williams, as for Helwys, a person should not be punished by civil magistrates for their religious beliefs, even if their religious beliefs are deemed heretical. Religious persecution, according to Williams, was expressly not a Christian concept.

Byrd has demonstrated that Roger Williams arrived at his views on religious liberty through his reading of the Bible. "In his published appeals for religious liberty," writes Byrd, "Williams quoted scripture incessantly, fully aware that the Bible was the authoritative basis for any argument that needed to persuade the widest possible audience."[16] The problem for Williams was that his opponents, those in favor of religious persecution, also argued their case from the Bible. The difference between Williams, who opposed religious persecution, and John Cotton, who favored religious persecution, was not that Williams read the philosophers and Cotton followed the Bible. Williams argued from the Bible but believed that his opponents had misinterpreted, and even perverted, it.[17]

Williams, writing in the American colonies decades after Helwys, seems to draw on English Baptists such as John Murton.[18] Byrd's notes, "In his interpretation of these passages, Williams likely appropriated the insights of some English Baptist writers, although they did not give the passages as much attention as Williams did."[19] This is not to say that Helwys, Murton, or Williams were monolithic in their approaches to religious liberty. However,

---

15 James P. Byrd, Jr., *The Challenges of Roger Williams: Religious Liberty, Violent Persecution, and the Bible* (Macon, GA: Mercer University Press, 2002), 1.
16 Byrd, *Challenges of Roger Williams*, 3.
17 Byrd, *Challenges of Roger Williams*, 4–5.
18 Roger Williams added Murton's *A Humble Supplication to the Kings Majesty* (1620) to the preface of his work *The Bloudy Tenent of Persecution* (1644).
19 Byrd, *Challenges of Roger Williams*, 148, n.50.

the connection does seem to demonstrate that both drew their arguments for religious liberty from the text of Scripture.

When Isaac Backus argued for religious toleration in the eighteenth-century American context, he did not argue primarily from the writings of Locke. Instead, he appealed to Scripture and the writings of Roger Williams who had likely been influenced by earlier English Baptists like John Murton.[20]

3. Conclusion

Thomas Helwys and Roger Williams represent early Protestant arguments for religious liberty that preceded the influence of Enlightenment philosophers such as John Locke. The two authors wrote on opposite sides of the Atlantic, and were influential in their respective locales. The primary point, however, is that religious toleration, as it developed in the early seventeenth century, was firmly rooted in the biblical text, not Enlightenment principles. Certainly, Locke exerted influence over American evangelicals in the eighteenth century. But Protestant arguments for religious toleration came long before Locke and were firmly anchored in the teachings of the Bible.

---

20 Coffey, "Puritanism and Liberty," 984.

"God Alone is Lord of the Conscience": A Commentary on Paragraph 2 of Chapter 21 of the 1689 Baptist Confession of Faith

Joseph Dunne, PhD

> Conscience itself is not a trustworthy rule. If a man's conscience be unenlightened, he may be sinning, and reaping the ill consequences of his sin, not less surely because he is not conscious that his misfortunes are due to his folly rather than his fate. His conscience cannot be the standard. The standard is the law of God.

—Charles Spurgeon in "A Clear Conscience" from the Metropolitan Tabernacle Pulpit, Vol. 24

1. Introduction

In the twenty-first chapter of the 1689 Baptist Confession of Faith, the second paragraph reads as follows:

> God alone is Lord of the conscience (Jas. 4:12; Rom. 14:4) and has left it free from the doctrines and commandments of men which are in any thing contrary to his word, or not contained in it. (Acts 4:19, 29; 1 Cor. 7:23; Matt. 15:9) So that to believe such doctrines, or obey such commands out of conscience, is to betray true liberty of conscience; (Col. 2:20, 22, 23) and the requiring of an implicit faith, an absolute and blind obedience, is to destroy liberty of conscience and reason also. (1 Cor. 3:5; 2 Cor. 1:24)

Central to this paragraph is the claim that "God alone is Lord of the conscience." But exactly what the signatories of this Confession intended to communicate with this phrase, and what it might mean to confess that lordship over the conscience belongs to God alone, may not be altogether clear upon an initial reading by most contemporary pastors and thinkers. So, to better understand this important confessional phrase, I will clarify each of its constituent parts for our modern context. To that end, this piece will seek to clarify three areas: (1) the nature of conscience and God's lordship over it, (2) the sense in which God is the Lord of conscience, and (3) what it means to confess that God alone is Lord of the conscience.

2. God Alone is Lord of the Conscience

Unfortunately, the Second London Baptist Confession of Faith never offers a formal definition of the concept of conscience. While the term "conscience" is invoked in 17.3, 18.1, 18.4, 21.2, and 24.3, it is nowhere explicitly defined. In the absence of a formal definition, however, we can nevertheless turn to some biblical and historical data on conscience to help clarify this otherwise ambiguous concept.

2.1 Biblical Data

Perhaps unsurprisingly, the phenomenon of conscience being invoked without being formally defined is true in the New Testament as well. Admittedly, the situation is even less clear in the Old Testament where the ancient Hebrews lacked a specific word for conscience altogether. Nevertheless, as Andrew Naselli and J. D. Crowley suggest: "the concept of conscience is certainly in the Old Testament even if no word itself is present."[1] Similarly, Richard Sorabji argues:

> Although the Hebrew Old Testament provides thrilling examples of what we should call conscience, notably in King David's remorse for acquiring Bathsheba by arranging the death of her husband, it used for conscience only the general word for heart, the seat of many different emotions. The few references to conscience in English versions of the Old Testament come from the ancient Greek translation of the Hebrew. This is not necessarily to say that the Hebrew writers lacked the concept. They could have had it without the word, and the Greeks may equally have supplied examples of moral conscience without the word.[2]

---

1   Andrew D. Naselli and J. D. Crowley, *Conscience: What It Is, How to Train It, and Loving Those Who Differ* (Wheaton, IL: Crossway, 2016), 33. In footnote 1 on page 33, Naselli and Crowley write: "Though the word conscience is rare in English translations of the Old Testament, the concept isn't uncommon. *Conscience* occurs in the Old Testament one time in the ESV and NASB (1 Sam. 25:31), four times in the NIV (Gen. 20:5, 6; 1 Sam. 25:31; Job 27:6; plus 'conscience-stricken' in 1 Sam. 24:5; 2 Sam 24:10), five times in the NET (Gen. 20:5, 6; 1 Sam. 24:5; 25:31; Job 27:6), and four times in the NLT (1 Sam. 24:5; 25:31; 2 Sam. 24:10; Job 27:6)."
2   Richard Sorabji, *Moral Conscience Through the Ages: Fifth Century BCE to the Present* (Chicago: The University of Chicago Press, 2014), 11.

The Old Testament example alluded to above where the concept of conscience is explored in the absence of the term is found in Ps. 51. Though the passage does not contain the term, John Cottingham believes that we can nevertheless discern a few noteworthy features of the concept of conscience from a cursory reading of the Psalm.

First, Cottingham thinks that David's conscience here displays a kind of self-directed disapproval toward his own actions that is "characteristically felt at the untoward behavior of another."[3] While our consciences can certainly disapprove of the perceived wrongdoings that abound around us, Cottingham's point here is that Psalm 51 highlights the self-evaluating nature of conscience that can similarly disapprove of the perceived wrongdoings that abound inside us as well.

Second, Cottingham notes that, as an otherwise seared conscience like David's becomes awakened, the resulting empathy and deepening self-evaluation produces guilt, remorse, and repentance. Just consider, for example, that once David is confronted for his sins by the prophet Nathan in 2 Sam. 12:1-15, David's "previously shallow grasp of the significance of his actions was altered under the imaginative stimulus of being presented with a vivid analogue of his own conduct, which made him start to appreciate how being treated in such a way would feel for the victim."[4] David's now awakened conscience directs the disapproval upon his own actions that he initially felt toward the perceived wrongdoings of the rich man in Nathan's story only after he self-identified with the man that Nathan was analogically speaking about. Once David's seared conscience awakens and convicts him of his sins, his empathy for his victims increases and so does his remorse for his actions—both of which then serve to motivate his repentance. Third and finally, Cottingham notes that David's repentance is not simply something "implanted from the outside by the prophet's condemnation but is partly elicited from within:" as the prophet Nathan helps to lift some of David's "emotional and cognitive barriers" by having him identify with the characters in his parable, "it is David's own conscience that convicts him."[5]

Another place in the Old Testament where we arguably see the concept of conscience being explored without invoking the term is in Psalm 32:1-4. In this Psalm, David offers a rich phenomenological exploration of what it is like to be subject to the oppression of a guilty conscience.

---

3   John Cottingham, "Conscience, Guilt, and Shame," in *The Oxford Handbook of The History of Ethics*, ed. Roger Crisp (Oxford: Oxford University Press, 2013), 731.
4   Cottingham, "Conscience, Guilt, and Shame," 731.
5   Cottingham, "Conscience, Guilt, and Shame," 731.

David does not characterize his guilty conscience as a *mere* belief about his moral blameworthiness but also uses strong bodily imagery to describe its consequences in his life as well—suggesting that conscience and its verdicts involve both cognitive and affective elements. He explains that, when he kept his iniquity silent and refused to acknowledge his wrongdoing, his bones felt like they were wasting away inside of him—so much so that he reports physically groaning all day long. He also interprets the weightiness of his guilty conscience as the Lord's heavy hand upon his body, drying up all of his physical strength just as the heat of summer can dry up all of our strength. David's imagery need not be merely metaphorical either. Contemporary empirical studies also confirm the same sort of embodied consequences of a guilty conscience that David poetically wrote about so long ago. These are: (1) a guilty conscience produces an increase in subjectively perceived body weight and an increase in the subjectively perceived effort needed to complete physically demanding behaviors;[6] and (2) that the "pricks" of conscience are associated with the sensation of physical pricks.[7]

With respect to the New Testament, Naselli and Crowley have offered a contemporary account of conscience that is based on the occurrences of the word *syneidēsis* ('conscience'). Therefore, they organize the New Testament data on conscience in the following way:

[Speaking about Conscience] *Positively*

The conscience can be good in the sense of blameless, clear, clean, and pure (Acts 23:1, 24:16; 1 Tim. 1:5, 19, 3:9; 2 Tim. 1:3; Heb. 13:18; 1 Pet. 3:16, 21).

---

6 Martin V. Day and D. Ramona Bobocel, "The Weight of a Guilty Conscience: Subjective Body Weight as an Embodiment of Guilt," PLoS ONE vol. 8(7): e69546 (July 31, 2013): 6, https://doi: 10.1371/journal.pone.0069546. They write: "Guilt is a common emotional experience following an unethical deed. Four studies revealed how actions that imbue feelings of guilt may be embodied and can affect judgments. Extending the metaphor that guilt is a heavy weight on people's conscience, Studies 1-3 demonstrated that immoral acts led to reports of increased subjective body weight compared to control conditions. Study 1 isolated the direction of the effect: unethical acts made participants feel heavier, but ethical acts did not make participants feel lighter. Studies 2 and 3 found that increased feelings of guilt can explain greater subjective weight, rather than feelings of disgust, pride, or sadness. Finally, Study 4 demonstrated that the same manipulation affected judgments consistent with the effects of physical weight. Physically demanding behaviors were perceived as more effortful to complete following recall of unethical as compared to ethical acts, thus indicating a consequence of the weight of guilt phenomenon."

7 Xyle Ku, Jonghwan Lee, and Hyunyup Lee, "Is Prick of Conscience Associated With the Sensation of Physical Prick?" *Frontiers in Psychology*, vol. 11, art. 283 (February 21, 2020): 7, https://doi: 10.3389/fpsyg.2020.00283. They write: "This study was conducted to investigate whether prick of conscience would be grounded in bodily experiences of physical prick (e.g., a needle prick), using a sample of Korean participants who were familiar with the metaphorical expression "It pricks my conscience." The results of the study lent support to our hypothesis that prick of conscience is associated with the physical sensation of pricking. Participants who recalled unethical acts (Study 1) and who lied (Study 2) appeared to become more sensitive to the needle prick than those who did not. In addition, participants who had the needle prick made more severe moral judgments than participants in the control condition (Study 3)."

The conscience can be cleansed, that is, cleared, perfected, purified, washed, purged, and sprinkled clean (Heb. 9:9, 14; 10:22).

[Speaking about Conscience] *Negatively*

The conscience can be weak (1 Cor. 8:7, 10, 12).

The conscience can be wounded (1 Cor. 8:12).

The conscience can be defiled (1 Cor. 8:7; Titus 1:15).

The conscience can be encouraged or emboldened to sin (1 Cor. 8:10).

The conscience can be evil or guilty (Heb. 10:22).

The conscience can be seared as with a hot iron (1 Tim. 4:2).[8]

Naselli and Crowley also contend that conscience performs the following three actions:

The conscience can bear witness or confirm (Rom. 2:15, 9:1; 2 Cor. 1:12, 4:2, 5:11).

The conscience can judge or try to determine another person's freedom (1 Cor. 10:29).

The conscience can lead one to act a certain way. The New Testament gives four examples: it can lead you either to accuse or defend yourself based on how your conscience bears witness (Rom. 2:15); it can lead you to submit to the authorities (Rom. 13:5); it can lead you not to bother asking where your meat came from because eating meat sacrificed to idols is not something your conscience should condemn you for (1 Cor. 10:25, 27); and it can lead you not to eat meat that someone tells you was sacrificed to idols for the sake of that person's conscience (1 Cor. 10:28).[9]

With their framework for the New Testament data in place, Naselli and Crowley conclude that conscience is best defined as "your consciousness of what you believe is right and wrong."[10] Insofar as conscience involves *beliefs*, Naselli and Crowley are sure to clarify that what we *believe* about right and wrong is not always the same as what *is* right and wrong. Thus, their description of conscience implies that it is both fallible and at least partly cognitive in nature insofar as conscience involves beliefs about right and wrong that can be true or false. Describing conscience in this way may help

---

8   Naselli and Crowley, *Conscience*, 40–41.

9   Naselli and Crowley, *Conscience*, 41–42. According to Naselli and Crowley, the verses containing the Greek term syneidēsis are as follows: Acts 23:1, 24:16; Rom. 2:15, 9:1, 13:5; 1 Cor. 8:7, 10, 12, 10:25, 27, 28, 29 (used twice); 2 Cor. 1:12, 4:2, 5:11; 1 Tim. 1:5, 19, 3:9, 4:2; 2 Tim. 1:3; Titus 1:15; Heb. 9:9b, 14, 10:2, 22, 13:18; 1 Pet. 2:19, 3:16, 21.

10 Naselli and Crowley, *Conscience*, 42.

explain, for example, why David could sleep at night with a clear conscience until the time of Nathan's confrontation: his clear conscience—that is, David's awareness of his otherwise false belief that he was morally blameless—was no accurate indication of whether he was, in fact, morally blameless before God. In other words, Nathan's rebuke of David demonstrates that having a clear conscience is not sufficient for being morally blameless.[11] Naselli and Crowley further contend that someone's clear conscience "may actually be evil because it is based on immoral standards."[12] However, in David's case, his disapproving reaction to the rich man in Nathan's analogical story seems to indicate that David's conscience was based on the proper moral standards that were simply not consciously applied to his own actions—for one reason or another.

Naselli and Crowley's New Testament account of conscience also helps to explain other features of David's story as well: what we might call the diversity or plurality of conscience's verdicts as well as its plasticity or changeability over time. On the one hand, Naselli and Crowley point out that conscience can produce different verdicts for different people insofar as their consciences are based on different moral standards. But as we've seen with David, the diverse verdicts of conscience can also result from some conscience applying its perhaps correct moral standards to others while failing to apply them to oneself. Moreover, the wide-ranging pluralism among consciences may also result from different consciences differently applying the same moral standards to similar situations as well. With respect to the plasticity of conscience, Naselli and Crowley first point out that our fundamental moral standards can—and often do—change over time. They also point out that consciences can—and often do—oscillate between various degrees of *oversensitivity* and *undersensitivity* through time—and even oscillate in this way relative to different topics as well. Naselli and Crowley explain that we can make conscience *insensitive* by "developing a habit of ignoring its voice of warnings so that the voice gets weaker and weaker and finally disappears" or make them *oversensitive* by

---

11 On this point, compare with Christopher Ash, *Discovering the Joy of a Clear Conscience* (Phillipsburg, NJ: P&R Publishing, 2014), 31–35: Far from being the voice of God inside of us, Ash contends that "conscience is an unreliable guide" insofar as it may lead you to "think you are innocent when you are guilty" or lead you to "think you are guilty when you have been forgiven." See also R. C. Sproul, *How Can I Develop a Christian Conscience?* (Sanford, FL: Reformation Trust Publishing, 2013), 7: Sproul argues that, "whereas God's principles don't change, our consciences vacillate and develop"—and these changes and vacillations "can be positive or negative" insofar as a conscience can come to "excuse when it ought to be accusing, and it also can accuse when it should be excusing."
12 Naselli and Crowley, *Conscience*, 42.

"packing it with too many rules that are actually matters of opinion, not right and wrong."[13]

2.2 Historical Data

Like the ancient Hebrews, the early Greeks likewise failed to have a specific term for conscience, but this did not mean that they lacked the concept either. In fact, Sorabji thinks that the early Greeks "may equally have supplied examples of moral conscience without [invoking] the word" insofar as the earliest basic conceptual expression that eventually came to be the standard term for conscience began to appear in the Greek playwrights of the fifth century BC.[14] This early expression involved the metaphor of one sharing knowledge with oneself, usually of a moral defect, as though one were split into two. The metaphor explains that when we possess knowledge of a moral defect—or possess a guilty conscience—it feels like we're split into two and composed of two different people: "one of them knows of the defect but is keeping it a secret; the other shares the secret—in cases of moral conscience, a guilty one."[15] Over time, who it is that the guilty knowledge was shared with would vary. But despite this, Sorabji argues that the meaning of the conscience metaphor "is at first unambiguous" and standardly "involves one's own knowledge of one's own fault."[16]

Sorabji explains that the basic split-self metaphor for conscience was eventually expressed terminologically—"by a particular form of the [Greek] verb for knowing, *suneidenai*, to share (*sun-*)knowledge (*eidenai*), coupled with the reflexive pronoun in the dative (e.g., *heautôi* [oneself])."[17] Fortunately, this Greek idiom concerning conscience would translate seamlessly into Latin: *con-* in the Latin noun *conscientia* is a simple translation of the Greek *sun-* and *scientia* is a simple translation of the Greek *eidêsis*. In Latin, therefore, *con* and *scientia* together yield *conscientia*—or sharing knowledge with oneself. It was by "strange good fortune," Sorabji points out, that "a literal translation, not a paraphrase, of the Greek term was used," which helped the Latin avoid "importing its own presuppositions into the very choice of word."[18]

---

13 Naselli and Crowley, *Conscience*, 29.
14 Sorabji, *Moral Conscience*, 11–12.
15 Sorabji, *Moral Conscience*, 12.
16 Sorabji, *Moral Conscience*, 12. See also C. A. Pierce, *Conscience in the New Testament* (London: SCM-Canterbury Press, 1955), 38.
17 Sorabji, *Moral Conscience*, 12.
18 Sorabji, *Moral Conscience*, 14.

Overall, Sorabji argues that the first 600 years of the conceptual development of conscience produced attributes which surprisingly remained fairly stable features over the next 2000 years:

1. Conscience is a form of *personal self-awareness* that is not invariably an awareness of *others*.
2. Conscience draws on values not necessarily shared by others.
3. Conscience originally involved the idea of a person split into two, with one self-hiding a guilty secret, and the other self-sharing it. The idea of conscience as involving a split person was to recur in different forms and with different rationales in Adam Smith, in Kant, and in Freud, and is found in the expression "I could not live with myself."
4. The original function of the conscience was retrospective, but very soon prospective functions developed and all of these were retained.
5. Although conscience drew on general values, it was very much concerned with what was or would be wrong for the *particular* individual in a *particular* context.
6. The concept of conscience started off secular, originating in the Greek playwrights of the fifth century BCE, and remains capable of being secular.
7. Conscience was traditionally viewed in Christianity as fallible.
8. Though a belief and hence cognitive in character, conscience nonetheless had motivating force.[19]

As noted, Sorabji thinks that, although the concept of conscience may have been subject to various interpretations since its genesis, it has nevertheless not required many revisions from its original picture. Though the history of the concept of conscience reveals at least two significant deviations from the basic structure developed in the first 600 years, these deviations did not last long. Whereas the first deviation was "the need to accommodate synderesis alongside conscience, which made one difference if synderesis took over the motivational role from conscience, or another difference if it relegated conscience to the act of drawing a conclusion rather than holding a belief," the second deviation "was the idea that conscience was a sentiment of approval or disapproval, or even a sensation of pain, rather than a belief or capacity for belief about what conduct or attitude was or would be wrong for one, a belief that might cause sentiments or pain."[20]

19 Sorabji, *Moral Conscience*, 36.
20 Sorabji, *Moral Conscience*, 215.

2.2.1 Conscience and Synderesis

The first deviation was most prominent in the Middle Ages and, according to Sorabji, arguably stemmed from Origen's interpretation of Ezekiel's vision of the four-faced creatures in Ezekiel 1:10. The creatures in this passage are described as having the face of a human, lion, ox, and eagle—and Origen interpreted the first three faces as corresponding to the three parts of Plato's tripartite soul. Whereas Origen interpreted the fourth part as "the human's spirit *(spiritus)* presiding over the other three," Jerome would later "refer the eagle to a fourth part, for which the Greeks have a name, and which is the 'spark of conscience' by which we recognize that we are sinning."[21] Therefore Jerome, likely drawing upon Origen, seemed to have mistakenly distinguished between conscience *(conscientia)* and the spark of conscience *(synderesis)*.[22]

Bonaventure would later distinguish between *conscientia* and *synderesis* as well, where the basis of his distinction was that conscience played a predominantly cognitive role and *synderesis* played a predominantly affective role.[23] As Douglas C. Langton notes, "Bonaventure regards conscience and synderesis as residing in different faculties: Conscience is part of the rational faculty, and synderesis is part of the affective. Yet, conscience and synderesis interpenetrate each other."[24] Similarly, Aquinas would distinguish between conscience and *synderesis* and give them different functions. Sorabji explains that, for Aquinas, *synderesis* supplied universal premises from the natural law and was "never mistaken, but in effect infallible."[25] Conscience, on the other hand, was simply the "act of applying the universal premise to a particular situation."[26] As opposed to Bonaventure, Aquinas would grant to conscience "no less than *synderesis* motivational force," believing that synderesis "warns, inclines, incites, and deters" and that conscience "can prospectively prod, urge, or bind, and retrospectively accuse or cause remorse."[27] Ultimately,

---

21 Sorabji, *Moral Conscience*, 59.
22 For a more detailed historical retracing of the origins of the distinction between conscience and *synderesis*, see Herman Bavinck, *Reformed Ethics: Created, Fallen, and Converted Humanity,* ed. John Bolt (Grand Rapids: Baker Academic, 2019), 177-181; Stuart P. Chalmers, *Conscience In Context: Historical and Existential Perspectives* (Bern, Switzerland: Peter Lang AG, International Academic Publishers, 2014), 71-89; Hendrik G. Stoker, *Conscience: Phenomenon and Theories,* trans. Philip E. Blosser (Notre Dame: Notre Dame Press, 2018), 35-43.
23 Sorabji, *Moral Conscience*, 61.
24 Douglas C. Langston, *Conscience and Other Virtues* (University Park, PA: Penn State University Press, 2001), 35. For more on Bonaventure's views of conscience and *synderesis*, see Chalmers, *Conscience*, 90-103; Langston, *Conscience*, 21-37.
25 Sorabji, *Moral Conscience*, 63.
26 Sorabji, *Moral Conscience*, 63-64.
27 Sorabji, *Moral Conscience*, 64. For more on Aquinas' views of conscience and *synderesis*, see Bavinck, *Reformed Ethics*, 180-181; Chalmers, *Conscience*, 124-150; Langston, *Conscience*, 39-51;

Sorabji claims that William of Ockham would dispense of synderesis on the basis of his famous Ockham's Razor—a trend that seemed to be upheld by the Protestant reformers Martin Luther (at least after 1519) and John Calvin.[28]

In the spirit of Ockham, Sorabji also believes that the division of labor between *synderesis* and conscience is not necessary for explaining motivation. He elaborates:

> For knowledge or belief is itself motivating, provided it is the knowledge or belief that some action would, or would not, be wrong for one to perform in an expected situation calling for decision. Bonaventure has found a task for synderesis to perform, but if I am right, the task could have been performed without it.[29]

Because he thinks that some beliefs can be sufficiently motivating in themselves—without the need for an additional, motivating capacity like *synderesis*—Sorabji argues that the Apostle Paul's simpler distinction between "the law in our hearts with its *general* knowledge of right and wrong [and] the conscience that accused or excused us as *individuals*" had already supplied all that was needed for conscience.[30] Finally, Sorabji also objects to Aquinas' account of conscience insofar as he does not believe that this capacity can recognize the law infallibly.

2.2.2 Conscience as Mere Sentiment

The second deviation was the idea that conscience was a sentiment of approval or disapproval, or even a sensation of pain, *rather than* a belief or capacity for belief about what conduct or attitude was or would be wrong for one—a belief that might cause sentiments or pain. This deviation can trace its roots back to the views of seventeenth and eighteenth century moral sentimentalists like Shaftesbury, Hutcheson, and Hume in addition to the later English philosopher J. S. Mill. Shaftesbury, for example, argued that we have "a natural sense of right and wrong," emphasizing that "our sense

Stoker, *Conscience*, 40–43.

28 Sorabji, *Moral Conscience*, 66. For more on Ockham's views of conscience and *synderesis*, see Langston 53–69. For more on Luther's views on conscience and synderesis, see Langston, *Conscience*, 71–84. For a broader overview of the Protestant and Reformed views on conscience, see Bavinck, *Reformed Ethics*, 181–189; Edward G. Andrew, *Conscience and Its Critics: Protestant Conscience, Enlightenment Reason, and Modern Subjectivity* (Toronto, Canada: University of Toronto Press, 2012), 12–33.

29 Sorabji, *Moral Conscience*, 61.

30 Sorabji, *Moral Conscience*, 65–66.

of right and wrong is a sense."[31] Hutcheson would agree with Shaftesbury, commonly speaking of "moral *sentiment,* and of the moral *sense,* which is *pleased or displeased by good or evil.*"[32] Likewise, Hume also spoke of a "moral *sense* and connected conscience with *passion* instead of *reason.*"[33] Mill would end up defining "the essence of conscience" as a "feeling in our own mind; a pain more or less intense, attendant on violation of duty"—showing that Mill also thought about conscience as a sensation.[34]

Contrary to the sentimentalists and Mill, Sorabji sees this position—that conscience is fundamentally a sentiment or sensation and not a belief or capacity for beliefs—as not only a historical derivation from the original concept, but a misguided view in its own right. Sorabji argues that a "sensation can indeed motivate, but if conscience is only a sensation, it will presumably be *produced by* value judgments about wrong, which are now no longer incorporated within conscience itself."[35] From Antiquity through the Middle Ages, the bites of conscience were understood as a "mere *effect* of bad conscience, with bad conscience itself being a belief about one's wrongdoing."[36] Relegating conscience to a mere sensation, then, would amount to equating it with what was once understood as an effect that it produced. So, even if one believes that conscience gives rise to sentiments and sensations of approval or disapproval as Sorabji does, such sentiments are better understood as the consequences of antecedent value judgments.

Sorabji concludes that the core, persisting conception of conscience through history that has become most influential contains the following attributes:

1. It is a person's *belief* about what actions or attitudes had been in the past, or would be in the future, wrong or not wrong for him to adopt or not adopt in a particular situation. It could also be the *capacity* for such beliefs. The beliefs may be the things believed or the believing of them.

2. The beliefs require *personal* self-awareness and are in the first instance beliefs about what would be wrong for *oneself.*

---

31 Sorabji, *Moral Conscience,* 168. For more on Shaftesbury's views of conscience, see Andrew, *Conscience,* 99-113.
32 Sorabji, *Moral Conscience,* 168-169.
33 Sorabji, *Moral Conscience,* 169. For more on Hutcheson and Hume's views of conscience, see Andrew, *Conscience,* 114-130.
34 Sorabji, *Moral Conscience,* 169. For more on Mill's views of conscience, see Andrew, 153-176.
35 Sorabji, *Moral Conscience,* 169.
36 Sorabji, *Moral Conscience,* 169.

3. Conscience is *motivating* because it is a *value* belief about what was or would be wrong for oneself. It can therefore cause both sentiments of approval or disapproval and painful or comforting sensations.

4. This connection with being in the *wrong* accounts for the *force* of, and respect for, conscience of others, for no one wants to be in the wrong. We do not have to look for something contingently and variably connected, such as its sometimes being central to people's identity, or causing intensity of feeling, or contributing to self-direction.

5. Conscience is acquired, not innate, not present from birth.

6. It draws on values which need not take the form of laws, but which are in danger of reflecting merely local convention, and therefore require constant reflection and awareness of other values.

7. It is not the voice of God, and its value does not depend on whether the values derive from God.

8. It is not infallible.

9. Conscience creates an obligation, but not always an overriding obligation, since there can be counter-obligations, so that one is in a double bind, wrong if one does follow conscience and wrong if one does not.

10. Freedom of conscience is the absence, within limits, of forcible constraint by authority not only on one's value beliefs, but also on the *actions* which those value beliefs forbid or require.

11. Freedom of conscience is a narrower term than toleration. Toleration can be recommended on many grounds besides the desirability of freedom of conscience, such as the need for peace.

12. Freedom of religion is not the same as freedom of conscience, but the two overlap and many of the same arguments can be given for both. Conscience, however, can be secular, and there are some advantages in its being so.

13. Freedom of conscience has different meanings.[37]

2.3 Synthesis

Given the various features of conscience discussed above I now will defend the broad conceptual compatibility of these accounts to highlight their shared set of core features. Taken together, I argue that they constitute a rough yet relatively stable notion of conscience that is informed by Scripture and the larger Christian tradition.

---

37 Sorabji, *Moral Conscience*, 217.

2.3.1 Conscience is Cognitive and Affective

For Naselli and Crowley, conscience is our consciousness of what we believe is right and wrong. When we compare this to the first feature of Sorabji's definition of conscience—namely, that it is a person's belief or else capacity to form beliefs about what actions or attitudes had been in the past, or would be in the future, wrong or not wrong for him to adopt or not adopt in a particular situation—their compatibility begins to come into view. Contrary to Sorabji, Naselli and Crowley only seem to highlight conscience beliefs in their definition without explicitly referencing conscience as a capacity. This does not mean, however, that their definition is incompatible with Sorabji's definition of conscience but may only reflect one aspect of his account—which remains agnostic about whether conscience refers specifically *to the things believed* or *to the believing of them*. A simple synthesis of their views could be as follows: *whereas conscience refers to the capacity to form value beliefs about what actions or attitudes had been in the past, or would be in the future, wrong or not wrong for us to adopt or not adopt in a particular situation, conscience beliefs just refer to these beliefs.* The case for the general compatibility of both accounts is strengthened when we emphasize the second feature of Sorabji's conscience in conjunction with the first: conscience beliefs require personal self-awareness and are in the first place beliefs about what would be wrong for oneself. Both definitions clearly emphasize that, at the very least, conscience involves *beliefs* and is, therefore, *cognitive* in nature. Additionally, their accounts also emphasize that we are aware or conscious of these beliefs concerning what actions or attitudes are right or wrong for us to adopt—either in the past, present or future—in a given situation as well.

Sorabji also argues that, although they are beliefs and therefore cognitive in nature, the beliefs of conscience are nevertheless motivating because they are *value beliefs* about what was or would be wrong for oneself. And these value beliefs of conscience are motivating, he says, because they can cause both sentiments of approval or disapproval and comforting or painful sensations—just as we saw in Psalm 32:1-4, for example. Sorabji thinks that the marriage of cognition and affection in conscience is made clearer when we consider that "rational knowledge of evaluative propositions about what is or is not wrong can itself be motivating, for example, if I know that some action to which I am tempted or which I have performed is *wrong*."[38]

---

38 Sorabji, *Moral Conscience*, 35. Compare this point with Geerhardus Vos, *Natural Theology*, trans. Albert Gootjes (Grand Rapids: Reformation Heritage Books, 2022), 68: "At its core, the conscience belongs to the intellectual faculty, and, more specifically, to the faculty of judgment. This is not, however, meant to deny that it can be joined with emotions or exercise influence on the will. The conscience is a judgment on things that are of the greatest importance to us, to which our emotion and will cannot remain indifferent."

Similarly, Naselli and Crowley argue that a major function of conscience is to judge us for how well we conform to the moral standards we endorse, making us feel guilt and pain relative to our conformity. Incidentally, contemporary theorists also seem to support what Langston refers to as this interpenetration of cognition and affection in conscience as well. For example, Patricia Churchland believes that the "verdict of conscience is not solely cognitive, moreover, but has two interdependent elements: *feelings* that urge us in a general direction, and *judgment* that shapes the urge into a specific action."[39] And, according to Paul Thagard and Tracy Finn, conscience is best understood as "a particular kind of emotional consciousness, produced by brain processes that combine cognitive appraisal with perception of bodily states."[40]

Finally, we can also point out that this view of conscience may help explain the two major historical deviations highlighted by Sorabji as well. Whereas the first deviation posited two separate capacities—namely, conscience and synderesis—in order to account for both cognitive and affective aspects of conscience respectively, the second deviation simply argued that conscience could not be cognitive and must be reductively sentimental or affective instead. However, if conscience does involve this dynamic interplay or interpenetration between cognition and affection, then it is easy to see how theorists might have been tempted to relegate each aspect to a separate capacity or else exalt one aspect as primary over, or more fundamental to, the other.

2.3.2 Conscience is Diverse and Neutral

Naselli and Crowley also claim that their account of conscience implies that conscience can, and oftentimes does, produce *different verdicts* for *different people* based on *different moral standards* and *different applications of the same or similar moral standards*. What they seem to be highlighting here is something that Sorabji also points out: that different people can hold vastly different conscience beliefs because they can endorse different moral values and apply them differently. Both Naselli and Crowley, as well as Sorabji, seem to understand conscience, therefore, not necessarily as the *supplier* of our values or moral standards, but instead as the *applier* of our values or moral standards. As Sorabji notes, "It is not conscience (at least not conscience

---

39 Patricia Churchland, *Conscience: The Origins of Moral Intuition* (New York: W. W. Norton & Company, 2019), 5.
40 Paul Thagard and Tracy Finn, "Conscience: What is Moral Intuition?" in *Morality and the Emotions*, ed. by Carla Bagnoli (Oxford: Oxford University Press, 2012), 150.

in the core sense) that has to *supply* our values in the first place. St. Paul ascribes the inner law to God; a secular view should agree that conscience is never the original source of our values, even though particular decisions of conscience can lead to new reflection on general values, without being their original source. Conscience rather *applies* values to the conduct and thoughts of the individual."[41] Conscience, rightly understood, is therefore a *value-neutral capacity* insofar as it applies our values or moral standards— whatever they might be and however we came to hold them—to our actions or attitudes to produce beliefs about how they measure up to those values or moral standards. And in the words of Naselli and Crowley, we might say that conscience guides us into conformity with whatever values or moral standards that we endorse, monitors and testifies to how well we're conforming to them, and judges us on our fidelity to them.[42]

Naselli and Crowley do seem to differ from Sorabji, however, in their belief that there is, in fact, some objectively correct set of moral standards or values for conscience to apply. In particular, they believe that the objectively correct set of moral standards or values are uniquely Christian values and the moral standards depicted in the Bible. To be fair, Sorabji might also believe that there is some objectively correct set of moral standards or values, but he stops short of claiming as much in developing his historical account of conscience. Nonetheless, this point seems fairly inconsequential given not only the value-neutrality of conscience, but also given the fact that we are concerned with developing an account of conscience (i.e., the *applier* of values) and not with developing an account of the source of values that conscience applies (i.e., the *supplier* of values). Further, Naselli and Crowley also seem to contend with Sorabji's fundamental secularity of conscience insofar as they believe that conscience originates with—and is actually a gift from—God who created us in his image and with this capacity.[43] However, God-given or not, the central nature and function of conscience remains largely consistent between the above accounts despite their differences concerning the origins of conscience and the values that it applies.

---

41 Sorabji, *Moral Conscience*, 218.
42 Naselli and Crowley, *Conscience*, 43: "...your conscience guides you to help you conform to moral standards, *monitors* how you conform to them, *testifies* to how you conform to them, and *judges* you for how you conform to them, thus making you feel guilt and pain."
43 For a contemporary defense of the theistic origins of conscience, see Tapio Puolimatka, "The Origin of Moral Conscience: Theistic Evolution versus Intelligent Design," in *Theistic Evolution: A Scientific, Philosophical, and Theological Critique*, eds. J. P. Moreland, Stephen C. Meyer, Christopher Shaw, and Wayne Grudem (Wheaton, IL: Crossway, 2017), 731–754.

2.3.3 Conscience is Fallible

Finally, both accounts also seem to agree that conscience is *fallible* and is in jeopardy not only of endorsing and applying bad values or immoral standards, but also of applying otherwise good values and moral standards in the wrong sort of way as well. Sorabji argues that the values that conscience ends up endorsing and applying are in great danger of merely reflecting local convention, and therefore require constant reflection, education, and awareness of other values. Sorabji thinks that this point may actually be the greatest criticism against conscience: that the values it applies to our actions may be entirely or else overly derived from custom or superstition.[44] Naselli and Crowley similarly identify the fallibility of conscience as such an important issue that they dedicate several chapters of their book offering practical advice about how to ameliorate and overcome conscience's fallibility, e.g., how to properly calibrate one's conscience, how to relate to other Christians and people from other cultures when your consciences disagree, and so on. Finally, it is also worth noting that both accounts point out that, given the fallibility of conscience, the values that it applies and the ways in which they are applied can, do, and should probably change over time.

That the conscience is fallible—at least in some sense or to some degree—is a conclusion that enjoys near universal support within the larger Christian tradition. Reflecting upon the apostle Paul's understanding of our fallible consciences, Sorabji writes:

> As with the original Greek concept, conscience in Paul is not the ultimate source of our knowledge of right and wrong. For him, the law in our hearts is the source. But conscience reveals our possession of that law. This makes the relationship between conscience and the inner law close, but not identity. Of course the inner law is faultless, but one's reading of it is fallible...The fallibility—not of the law, but—of conscience remained the normal Christian view.[45]

---

44 Sorabji, *Moral Conscience*, 220.

45 Sorabji, *Moral Conscience*, 31-33. It is also worth noting that chapter twenty-one of the 1689 Baptist Confession of Faith curiously makes no reference to God's law written on the human heart—or any kind of other moral truth or norm discernible in general revelation—and its relationship to the conscience. However, in chapter nineteen, the moral law of God written on the heart of man is greatly explored. There we read in 19.1 that "God gave to Adam a law of universal obedience written on his heart" and in 19.2 that this "same law that was first written in the heart of man continued to be a perfect rule of righteousness after the fall..." From 19.3, we see that, commonly "called moral," this law "does for ever bind all" as described in 19.5 and informs us of "the will of God and [our] duty" as described in 19.6. Moreover, we also know from 1.1 that,"although the light of nature, and the works of creation and providence do so far manifest the goodness, wisdom, and power of God, as to leave men inexcusable; yet they are not sufficient to give that knowledge of God and His will which is necessary unto salvation." Thus, the will of God and our duties that the moral law informs

Similarly, as a contemporary voice offering commentary on the larger Christian tradition, Herman Bavinck is also careful to distinguish between our fallible consciences and the infallible law that conscience interprets.[46] Bavinck explains that conscience "forms a judgment in accordance with that law of God which lies elsewhere (in the heart)"—not judging "the true and false as such, but judg[ing] about the good and evil of the person's being."[47] As Bavink points out, the judgments of conscience arguably concern "everything in a person, about the entire person; not merely about our actions but also about our being and state and our thoughts" because "in our whole person we always stand before the law" and also because "nothing in us or done by us is outside the law."[48] Even so, as a "judge in God's name," Bavinck is clear that—at least as taught by Scripture and experience—the conscience "does not exercise its function infallibly."[49] Our conscience simply judges whether, and to what extent, we are living in accordance with God's law and will.[50] And while the law and will of God may be unchanging, our knowledge and interpretation of that otherwise perfect and immutable law can be imperfect, fallible, and impure as a result of distorting factors like immaturity, moral underdevelopment, and sin's corruption.[51]

With the above features of conscience now demarcated, consider the following attempt at a synthesized definition of conscience for the remaining purpose of interpreting the Confession:

> Conscience: *the capacity to form value beliefs concerning the sorts of things about us as persons that have been in the past, or will be in the present or future, wrong or not wrong.*

---

us about in chapter nineteen must concern the *non-salvific* will of God and our *moral duties*. The central point here is just that omitting any discussion about the conscience and its relationship to the moral law may strike us as odd, given that one of the primary functions of conscience is to fallibly draw upon and fallibly apply the norms of the moral law written upon our hearts—thereby informing us of things like the non-salvific will of God and our moral duties—to everything about us as persons.

46 Bavinck, *Reformed Ethics*, 175: "...conscience is not identical with the law nor the seat of the law."

47 Bavinck, *Reformed Ethics*, 194.

48 Bavinck, *Reformed Ethics*, 201-202.

49 Bavinck, *Reformed Ethics*, 208.

50 See also Ash, *Conscience*, 19-20: Conscience is defined as "...a self-awareness, a reflective faculty within myself that enables me to reflect upon myself..[enabling] me to think about the rightness or wrongness of my words, actions and thoughts...[by taking] the universal principles of right and wrong that I know, and [applying] them to my particular circumstances."

51 Bavinck, *Reformed Ethics*, 174: "...the conscience provides the judgment of human beings about themselves in their existing relationship to God, his law, and his will. That law and will of God—in other words, God himself—in relation to which people consider themselves bound in their conscience and in terms of which they evaluate themselves in their conscience, is unchanging and remains eternally the same. But that law can change within the subject's conscience itself, according to the subject's level of development, moral nurture, and knowledge; that is to say, the conscience can interpret and impurely reflect that law, which itself is immutable. That results from the conscience itself being impure, corrupted by sin."

With respect to the Confession, recall that 21.2 speaks of conscience as being "free from the doctrines and commandments of men." With this phrase, the Confession speaks to how our consciences should be free from adopting—and therefore free from applying to our persons—those problematic doctrines and commandments of mere men. Most centrally, therefore, the Confession seems to speak about freeing our consciences from some form of false or wayward captivity. With the above analysis of conscience in place, we can better appreciate at least two aspects of the conscience related to what the Confession highlights with this phrase: (1) that our otherwise fallible consciences can be captivated by the *wrong* sorts things; and (2) that our consciences can accuse, condemn, exonerate, or acquit us about *everything* from doctrines that we do or do not believe to commandments that we do or do not obey. In other words, by providing a clear definition of the *nature* of conscience, we may be able to better understand how we could speak about the conscience as being free from or captive to everything from problematic doctrines to the problematic commandments of mere men. As a *fallible* capacity, the value beliefs that conscience produces as a result of applying our values to our persons can be mistaken: its accusations and condemnations can offer a false captivity while its exonerations and acquittals can offer a false freedom. And as a capacity that evaluates *everything* about us as persons, the value beliefs that conscience produces in us can falsely accuse, condemn, exonerate, or acquit us about everything from doctrines believed or not to commandments obeyed or not. So, with the nature of conscience clarified, and some commentary on the latter part of the first sentence of 21.2 provided, we now turn to clarifying the nature of God's *lordship* over the conscience insofar as the first part of the first sentence of 21.2 confesses that "God alone is Lord of the conscience."

3. God Alone is *Lord* of the Conscience

In a basic sense, you might think that God is the proper *Lord* of our consciences insofar as he is the ultimate author and creator of the capacity. While this may be true, some have offered much richer accounts of God's lordship that entail more than mere authorship or creation. For example, John Frame has suggested that God's lordship can be properly understood through a threefold set of *lordship attributes,* including *control, authority,* and *presence.* With respect to control, Frame explains that God as Lord "controls the entire course of nature and history for his own glory and to accomplish his own purposes."[52] Second, Frame contends that, whereas control means "that God has the power to direct the whole course of nature and history as he pleases," God's lordship attribute of authority "means that he has the right to do that."[53] As such, God as Lord is both the "supreme controller of the world [and] its supreme evaluator."[54] Finally, Frame describes God's third lordship attribute of presence as his ability "to act on and in the creation and to evaluate authoritatively all that is happening in the creation"—and doing so "as present as an incorporeal being can be."[55]

Applying the lordship attributes of control, authority, and presence to the ethical life in particular, Frame writes:

> First, by his control, God plans and rules nature and history so that certain human acts are conducive to his glory and others are not. Second, by his authority, he speaks to us clearly, telling us what norms [should] govern our behavior. Third, by his covenant presence, he commits himself to be with us in our ethical walk, blessing our obedience, punishing our disobedience.[56]

Similarly, Frame indicates that God's lordship over the realm of *human knowledge* would entail that "the highest rules or norms of knowledge come from him, [that] the course of nature and history is under control, so that the facts are his facts, [and that] our knowledge faculties are gifts of God and operate in his very presence."[57] Applying Frame's lordship attributes to the conscience, then, God alone would be Lord of the conscience insofar as he exercised control, authority, and presence over it. As Lord of the conscience, therefore, we might say that God controls nature and history so that certain human acts of conscience are conducive to his glory and purposes while others are not. Moreover, we might say God is the supreme evaluator, judge, or arbiter of the conscience. And finally, we might also say that God is Lord of the conscience insofar we understand this faculty as a divine gift that always operates in the presence of God who blesses our obedience and punishes disobedience as well.

---

52 John H. Frame, *Systematic Theology: An Introduction to Christian Belief* (Phillipsburg, NJ: P&R Publishing, 2013), 21.
53 Frame, *Systematic Theology*, 22.
54 Frame, *Systematic Theology*, 22.
55 Frame, *Systematic Theology*, 29.
56 Frame, *Systematic Theology*, 1102.
57 Frame, *Systematic Theology*, 32.

4. *God* Alone is Lord of the Conscience

Thankfully, we are not troubled with the same sort of unclarity on this next point that we were with the question about the nature of conscience. Remember that the Confession says that "*God* alone is the Lord of the conscience and has left it free from the doctrines and commandments of men which are in any thing contrary to *his word*, or not contained in *it*." A cursory reading seems to suggest, then, that the lordship of God over the conscience—that is, his *authoritative* lordship—is exercised through his word. And by "his word," the Confession refers specifically to *God's word understood as God's authoritative written words given to us in the Bible*. For example, 1.2 of the Confession declares that "Under the name of *Holy Scripture, or the Word of God written,* are now contained all the books of the Old and New Testaments." (emphasis added) Connecting God's written words to God's authoritative lordship, 1.4 contends that "The *authority of the Holy Scripture,* for which it ought to be believed, depends not upon the testimony of any man or church, but wholly upon God (who is truth itself), the author thereof; therefore it is to be received *because it is the Word of God."* (emphases added) And finally, 1.10 concludes that "The supreme judge, by which all controversies of religion are to be determined, and all decrees of councils, opinions of ancient writers, doctrines of men, and private spirits, are to be examined, and in whose sentence we are to rest, *can be no other but the Holy Scripture* delivered by the Spirit, into which Scripture so delivered, our faith is finally resolved." (emphasis added)

Moving forward, we can now ask: what might it mean to say that God has left our consciences "free from the doctrines and commandments of men which are in any thing contrary to his word, or not contained in it?" On the one hand, it seems clear that the Confession believes it is *morally impermissible* for our consciences to endorse any doctrine or commandment that is contrary to God's word—either explicitly or implicitly. Conversely, while it may nevertheless be true that it is *morally obligatory* for our consciences to endorse every doctrine and commandment that is either explicitly or implicitly found in God's word, we should note that the Confession stops short of straightforwardly stating this (otherwise true) positive claim in this chapter and paragraph. On the other hand, just how we should understand the other disjunct at the end of this phrase—"or not contained in it"—is not as clear in comparison. You might think that, by being free from the doctrines and commandments of men, that it is morally *non-obligatory (or morally omissible)* for our consciences to endorse such things. However, this raises further puzzles insofar as the deontic notion of moral non-obligatoriness (or moral omissibility) can either mean *morally optional* or *morally impermissible*. So, we can ask: does the Confession suggest that it is morally optional or morally impermissible for our consciences to endorse the doctrines and commandments of men not contained within the word of God?

I think the answer can plausibly be *both*. In a more straightforward reading, the Confession suggests that binding our consciences to the doctrines and commandments of men not contained in the Bible would be morally impermissible insofar as this involves something like asking or requiring "someone to obey our commands *as if they were the commands of God himself* (absolutely)"—and does so *"without scriptural proof* that they are (blindly)."[58] Surely we can agree that endorsing man-made doctrines and commandments not found in the Bible as if they were God-given is morally impermissible in and of itself. And we can also agree that doing so without scriptural proof, thereby requiring an "implicit faith" or an "absolute and blind obedience," would likewise be *morally impermissible*—not least of which because asking or requiring someone to do so would "destroy...reason" by asking or requiring that they believe and act without reason. In light of these claims, therefore, we can affirm alongside the Confession that it is morally impermissible for our consciences to endorse the doctrines and commandments of men not contained in the Bible *as if they were the commands of God*—and perhaps doubly impermissible to do so *blindly and without reason*.

However, it also seems fair to say that, insofar as we do not endorse man-made doctrines and commandments not contained in the Bible *as if* they were God-given (much less that we do so blindly), it is morally optional to endorse them. That is, we seem free to endorse such man-made doctrines and commandments not contained in the Bible provided they are not explicitly or implicitly contrary to God's word—and provided we do not elevate them to a God-given status—but instead endorse them with something like a comparatively lesser authority, weightiness, or bindingness. If this claim about optionality is correct, then it seems possible to interpret the Confession as saying that it is *both* morally optional *and* morally impermissible for our consciences to endorse the doctrines and commandments of men not contained within the word of God—and that the difference between them trades on whether or not our consciences endorse the doctrines and commandments of men as God-given. Such a conclusion preserves the central meaning, for example, of the oft-quoted phrase that

---

58 Sam Waldron, *A Modern Exposition of the 1689 Confession* (Darlington, UK: Evangelical Press, 1989), 261; emphasis added.

nothing is *truly* considered sin by God that is not forbidden by Scripture (either explicitly or implicitly) and that nothing is truly required of us by God that is not commanded in Scripture (either explicitly or implicitly).

5. God *Alone* is Lord of the Conscience

Finally, we arrive at the last juncture in our quest to better understand 21.2 of the 1689 Baptist Confession of Faith: what might it mean to say that God *alone* is Lord of the conscience? In light of what has been concluded above, we might say that God *alone* is Lord of the conscience insofar as *God's word alone is the supremely authoritative arbiter or judge of our value beliefs concerning the sorts of things about us as persons that have been or will be wrong or not wrong.* That the word of God alone is the supremely authoritative evaluator of the conscience helps explain why the Confession says: (1) that it is morally impermissible for our consciences to endorse any doctrine or commandment that is contrary to God's word; (2) that it is morally impermissible for our consciences to endorse the doctrines and commandments of men not contained in the Bible as if they were the commands of God—especially if they are endorsed blindly and without reason; and (3) that it is morally optional to endorse the doctrines and commandments of men not contained in the Bible provided we do not endorse them as if they were God-given.

Therefore, we might say that God's word *alone* is the Lord of the conscience insofar as God's word is the *only final* or *highest* authority that we should appeal to when judging or arbitrating the evaluations of conscience. In this way, God's word is plausibly understood as the *norma normans non normata*—or "the norming norm that is not normed"—while the conscience is plausibly understood as the norma normata—"or the norm that is normed." Yet, to say that God's word is the *only final* or *highest* authority when evaluating the evaluations of conscience would not imply that God's word is the *only* or *sole* authority when evaluating the evaluations of conscience—a position commonly described as *nuda Scriptura*. As Matthew Barrett points out, "[t]hose who sing *this* mantra believe that creeds, confessions, the voices of tradition, and those who hold ecclesiastical offices carry no authority in the church. But this was not the Reformers' position, nor should it be equated with *sola Scriptura*."[59] Indeed, to endorse *nuda Scriptura* with respect to the relationship between God's word and the conscience—i.e., God's word is the *only* or *sole* authority over the

---

59 Matthew Barrett, *God's Word Alone: The Authority of Scripture* (Grand Rapids: Zondervan, 2016), 23.

conscience—as opposed to *sola Scriptura*—i.e., God's word is the *only final* or *highest* authority over the conscience—would doubtlessly be an ironic position for a Confession like this to articulate.

We can conclude this section, then, by affirming God's word as the only final or highest authority over the conscience while denying that God's word is the only or sole authority over the conscience. Or, as Article II of the *Chicago Statement on Biblical Inerrancy* states: "We affirm that the Scriptures are the *supreme* written norm by which God binds the conscience, and that the authority of the Church is subordinate to that of Scripture. We deny that Church creeds, councils, or declarations have authority *greater than* or *equal to* the authority of the Bible." (emphases added) And as 1.1 and 1.10 of the Confession say: "The Holy Scripture is the only sufficient, certain, and infallible rule of all saving knowledge, faith, and obedience" and is likewise the "supreme judge, by which all controversies of religion are to be determined, and all decrees of councils, opinions of ancient writers, doctrines of men, and private spirits, are to be examined, and in whose sentence we are to rest..." Therefore, we can conclude that, roughly, *God's word alone—affirmed as the only final or highest authority over the conscience and over every other authority—is the supremely authoritative arbiter or judge of our value beliefs concerning the sorts of things about us as persons that have been or will be wrong or not wrong.* Perhaps this best articulates what the 1689 Baptist Confession of Faith means when it so clearly and confidently declares that "God alone is Lord of the conscience."

Spurgeon, Temperance, and Christian Liberty

Geoff Chang, PhD

1. Introduction

Beginning in America in the 1820s, the temperance movement became a major force across the English-speaking world, reaching the British Isles by the end of the century. Early advocates of the temperance movement fought for the elimination of hard liquor, rather than beer or wine. But by 1833, a stricter form of temperance known as teetotalism arose, advocating for a total abstinence from all alcoholic beverages. Soon, this came to be the dominant position of the temperance movement. It would grow, so that by the middle of the nineteenth century, there were numerous temperance societies promoting these ideas among the working class, children, women, and in foreign lands. Not surprisingly, the temperance movement found religious support both in the Established Church and among Dissenting groups. According to some estimates, by the end of the nineteenth century, about a tenth of the adult population was committed to teetotalism.[1]

When young Charles Haddon Spurgeon (1834–1892) arrived at the New Park Street Chapel in London in 1854, the temperance movement was a part of his religious landscape. Many in his church-going audience were committed to the cause. Though he was not a teetotaler, Spurgeon was sympathetic. Prior to London, he pastored in a village that was notorious for drunkenness. As a pastor, he encountered first-hand the ruin that alcohol could bring, not only to the individual but also to the family.

At the same time, Spurgeon knew that he had been called to preach the gospel, not to promote temperance. For many Christian temperance advocates, teetotalism was beginning to take priority over the work of the gospel. One evidence of this was the growing division over these issues, even among Christians. "To make men sober is one thing, to make them quarrelsome is

---

1   For a history of the temperance movement in Britain see Brian Howard Harrison, *Drink and the Victorians: The Temperance Question in England, 1815–1872* (Pittsburgh: University of Pittsburgh Press, 1971).

another."[2] As the pastor of a church that held to the 1689 Baptist Confession of Faith and Keach's Solemn Covenant, the church did not have an official position on alcohol. Beyond a commitment "to walk in all holiness, godliness, humility, and brotherly love," this was a congregation open both to teetotalers and to those who drank in moderation. Therefore, Spurgeon was committed to promoting Christian liberty and unity, even as he held strong personal views on the temperance movement.

2. Spurgeon and the Temperance Movement

Preaching to an audience of over 23,000 people for the Fast-Day Service in 1857, Spurgeon called them to repent from the many sins of English society, including drunkenness:

> I am no total abstainer —I do not think the cure of England's drunkenness will come from that quarter. I respect those who thus deny themselves, with a view to the good of others, and should be glad to believe that they accomplish their object. But though I am no total abstainer, I hate drunkenness as much as any man breathing, and have been the means of bringing many poor creatures to relinquish this beastial indulgence. We believe drunkenness to be an awful crime and a horrid sin; we look on all its dreadful effects, and we stand prepared to go to war with it, and to fight side by side with abstainers, even though we may differ from them as to the mode of warfare.[3]

As a 23-year-old, Spurgeon made it clear that he was no teetotaler. However, that issue was secondary. The main issue was the war against the sin of drunkenness itself. There could be disagreement about the best way to go about fighting this war, whether by promoting total abstinence or by taking a more moderate position, but both groups should be ready "to fight side by side" against drunkenness.

As one who drank in moderation, there is no evidence that Spurgeon ever succumbed to drunkenness, which would've been a scandal for any pastor. In his day, drinking was a normal part of society, even among Christians. Liquor was commonly served at breaks during Baptist associational meetings and members regularly gave him bottles of wine as gifts. To refuse to drink in a social setting was impolite, even offensive. Spurgeon had no conscientious objection to participating in these social norms during the first decade of

---

2   C.H. Spurgeon, ed. *The Sword and the Trowel; A Record of Combat with Sin & Labour for the Lord*, Vol. 12 (London: Passmore & Alabaster, 1876), 45.

3   C.H. Spurgeon, *The New Park Street Pulpit: Containing Sermons Preached and Revised by the Rev. C. H. Spurgeon, Minister of the Chapel.* Vol. 3, (Pasadena, TX: Pilgrim Publications, 1975–1991), 344.

his ministry. In his sermons, he preached against drunkenness, but he also warned teetotalers not to place their hope in their abstinence but in Christ alone.

But in 1865, he began to change his mind on the issue. He was present when his nine-year-old twin sons received the Band of Hope's "medallion of membership," a pledge of their commitment to teetotalism.[4] Given his support of his sons, word began to spread that Spurgeon himself had also committed to teetotalism, and many in the temperance movement rejoiced. It's not clear if Spurgeon ever made those commitments public, but in time, he found that he could not keep his commitment and returned to a moderate position. Initially, he claimed use of wine was only "as a medicine," but eventually, he decided that he was free to "take them as a beverage." One American pastor, Justin Fulton, visited him in 1868 and sadly confirmed that "he had gone back to the use of beer and wine."[5] He urged teetotalers to pray for Spurgeon's recommitment to their cause.

From that time, Spurgeon had an uneasy relationship with the temperance movement. He continued to see drunkenness as a societal ill, but he found it harder to partner with those who required total abstinence. Commenting in 1876 on the Tabernacle's use of fermented wine at the Lord's Table, Spurgeon wrote:

> As the slightest word on this subject generally brings a flood of angry letters, we beg to intimate that our columns are not open to discussion, and that our own mind is made up. We are at one with those temperate temperance friends who forbear to divide churches, and mar the unity of the saints upon this point: to them we wish God speed, and we hope ever to cooperate with them.[6]

Spurgeon lamented those in the teetotaling camp who refused to cooperate with any who held a different view. Such a position divided the churches and marred the unity of the saints.

3. Smoking to the Glory of God

Over time, the temperance movement expanded not only to address drinking, but also smoking. The two often went together, and the addictive

4   C.H. Spurgeon, *C.H. Spurgeon's Autobiography: Compiled from His Diary, Letters, and Records, by His Wife, and His Private Secretary.* Vol. 3, (London: Passmore & Alabaster, 1897), 276-277.
5   Justin D. Fulton, *Spurgeon Our Ally* (Brooklyn, NY: The Pauline Propaganda, 1923), 264, 266.
6   C.H. Spurgeon, ed. *The Sword and the Trowel; A Record of Combat with Sin & Labour for the Lord*, Vol. 12 (London: Passmore & Alabaster, 1876), 45.

nature of tobacco also proved to be destructive, especially among the young and the poor. Many in the temperance movement who began as teetotalers eventually took the further step of abstaining from tobacco.

Spurgeon, however, had enjoyed smoking ever since his teenage years and had a reputation for being a cigar smoker. All this came to a head in 1874, when George Pentecost, an American temperance advocate, went on tour in the UK and visited the Metropolitan Tabernacle. During an evening service, Spurgeon invited Pentecost to make a few comments. Pentecost got up and spoke "fiercely against the sin of smoking tobacco, especially in the form of cigars, and told his hearers how he had struggled and fought against the pernicious habit, and how at last, by the blessing and with the assistance of Providence, he had conquered his addiction to the weed."[7] Spurgeon then took the platform. As the pastor of the church and as one who smoked, he felt compelled to speak. One magazine reported the following comments:

> Well, dear friends, you know that some men can do to the glory of God what to other men would be sin. And notwithstanding what brother Pentecost has said, I intend to smoke a good cigar to the glory of God before I go to bed to-night.
>
> If anybody can show me in the Bible the command, "Thou shalt not smoke," I am ready to keep it; but I haven't found it yet. I find ten commandments, and it's as much as I can do to keep them; and I've no desire to make them into eleven or twelve.
>
> The fact is, I have been speaking to you about real sins, not about listening to mere quibbles and scruples. At the same time, I know that what a man believes to be sin becomes a sin to him, and he must give it up. "Whatsoever is not of faith is sin" [Rom. 14:23], and that is the real point of what my brother Pentecost has been saying.
>
> Why, a man may think it a sin to have his boots blacked. Well, then, let him give it up, and have them whitewashed. I wish to say that I'm not ashamed of anything whatever that I do, and I don't feel that smoking makes me ashamed, and therefore I mean to smoke to the glory of God.[8]

There was an immediate backlash from those in the temperance movement. The press was quite happy to report this incident and highlight Spurgeon's comment about smoking "to the glory of God." One critic wrote to say that he had been helping his son battle his addictions, but because of Spurgeon's comments, the son had returned to smoking. Another critic, W. M. Hutchings, wrote a lengthy tract against Spurgeon, seeing him as a threat

---

7   *The Daily Telegraph*, September 23, 1874.
8   *Christian World*, September 25, 1874.

to the growing temperance movement. Spurgeon eventually had to publish something of an apology for his words.[9]

Nevertheless, Spurgeon's concern was pastoral. He was not primarily defending cigar smoking but was concerned about a Christian's liberty of conscience. Rather than adding to Scripture, he wanted to focus on matters which are "real sins," not just "mere quibbles and scruples." At the same time, Spurgeon recognized the importance of the conscience and provided instruction on that subject. In the end, Spurgeon believed that smoking in itself was not a sin, and he did not want to forbid what Scripture did not.[10]

Amid this ordeal, Spurgeon wrote to a friend and confessed, "What a badgering I have gone through! But I yield not, for what I said was right. There is no liberty left us by these spiritual prudes... If we cannot live near to God and smoke, we must give it up. I can and shall not confess to the contrary, not even by silence."[11] Even as he fought against drunkenness, Spurgeon was also ready to fight for Christian liberty. During these years, as one who held to a moderate position, Spurgeon found himself fighting the battle on both fronts.

4. Spurgeon the Teetotaler

However, by 1880, Spurgeon had recommitted himself to teetotalism. Preaching on the wedding at Cana, Spurgeon argued that the wine Jesus miraculously created was not nearly as "poisonous" as the liquor that was commonly sold in his day. "The kind of wine which he made was such that, if there had been no stronger drink in the world, nobody might have thought it necessary to enter any protest against drinking it." Then he declared, "I abstain myself from alcoholic drink in every form, and I think others would be wise to do the same; but of this each one must be a guide unto himself."[12] It's unclear exactly when he made the transition, but for the rest of his life, Spurgeon abstained from alcohol as a beverage and only took it medicinally,

---

9 "You cannot regret more than I do the occasion which produced the unpremeditated remarks to which you refer." Spurgeon went on to explain and defend his remarks, but the Editor of the *Daily Telegraph* did not accept this "apology." Fulton, *Spurgeon Our Ally*, 346.

10 "As I would not knowingly live even in the smallest violation of the law of God, and sin is the transgression of the law, I will not own to sin when I am not conscious of it. There is growing up in society, a Pharisaic system which adds to the commands of God the precepts of men; to that system I will not yield for an hour. The preservation of my liberty may bring upon me the upbraidings of many of the good, and the sneers of the self-righteous; but I shall endure both with serenity, so long as I feel clear in my conscience before God." Fulton, *Spurgeon Our Ally*, 346.

11 C.H. Spurgeon to John MacGregor "Rob Roy," from The Spurgeon Library Collection, Kansas City, MO.

12 C.H. Spurgeon, *The Metropolitan Tabernacle Pulpit: Sermons Preached and Revised by C. H. Spurgeon.* Vol. 26 (Pasadena, TX: Pilgrim Publications, 1970–2006), 494.

as prescribed by his doctor.[13] By 1886, the church discontinued the use of fermented wine at the Lord's Supper and switched over to "the fruit of the vine." What brought about this change?

Critics believed that Spurgeon's transition to teetotalism was entirely pragmatic, due to his health struggles, particularly gout. But those in the temperance movement argued that through friendships with temperance advocates like John B. Gough and others, Spurgeon became convinced of their position. He was particularly concerned for the havoc that alcohol caused among poor communities. It's impossible to know the full motivation behind this transition, but the answer is probably somewhere in between.

After 1880, as a teetotaler, Spurgeon was invited to speak at temperance gatherings and his lectures reveal strong convictions about his position. Undoubtedly, he continued to see drunkenness as a great social evil, and he brought all his homiletical powers to bear against it. At the same time, he was careful in his message to moderates. Rather than demanding all Christians to become teetotalers, he framed it as a challenge for their consideration. Regarding drinking, Spurgeon exhorted, "Try to reduce the mischief that you do to a minimum. Do as little as possible, and when you get down to that minimum, I should not wonder if it evaporate into nothing at all." At the same time, even if they were unconvinced, he called moderates not to sneer at the teetotalers, but to support them in their efforts against drunkenness.[14] As before, his concern was for both groups to work together.

On March 15, 1882, the Metropolitan Tabernacle established a new institution, namely the Metropolitan Tabernacle Gospel Temperance Society. Here, members of the church and the surrounding community signed a pledge and donned a blue ribbon, indicating their commitment to teetotalism. Spurgeon, due to illness, was not able to attend their founding meeting. However, he wrote a letter expressing his support, "I sincerely believe that, next to the preaching of the gospel, the most necessary thing to be done in England is to induce our people to become total abstainers." In saying this, Spurgeon did not disconnect the preaching of the gospel from the cause of abstinence but saw the two working together. He urged his church:

> I hope this Society will do something when it is started. I don't want you to wear a lot of peacocks' feathers and patty medals, nor to be always trying to convert the moderate drinkers, but

---

13 Spurgeon never gave up smoking, however.
14 C.H. Spurgeon, *Drinking and Abstinence* (New York: National Temperance Society and Publication House, 1883), 10–11.

to go in for winning the real drunkards, and bringing the poor enslaved creatures to the feet of Jesus, who can give them liberty.[15]

Here was the heart of Spurgeon's teetotalism. It was not ultimately about converting people to a particular position on temperance. It was about bringing those lost to the sin of drunkenness to the feet of Jesus. Like all other institutions of the Tabernacle, the Gospel Temperance Society was an evangelistic ministry. At the one-year anniversary of the institution, Spurgeon reported:

> The friends who manage the society do not intend it to become a temperance work with a little gospel tagged on; but they are resolved to put as much as possible of Christ and free grace into all efforts on behalf of sobriety and abstinence. It is something to wash the blackamoors of drunkenness, but our hearts can never rest till grace makes them white once for all.[16]

By the end of his life, Spurgeon had become a teetotaler and a strong advocate for the temperance movement. But he never lost sight of the gospel. Even as he promoted temperance to his people, he maintained the priority of the gospel and the unity of the church:

> You may go to them and plead the cause of temperance with them, and I hope you will; the more of it, the better. Make teetotalers of every one of them if you can, for it will be a great blessing to them; but still, you have not really done anything permanent if you stop there. Try the gospel! Try the gospel! Try the gospel![17]

5. Conclusion

Spurgeon's relationship with the temperance movement provides a fascinating case study into his approach to Christian liberty. As is evident by the cigar on display in the Spurgeon Library on the campus of Midwestern Seminary, many people today see Spurgeon as a champion of the Christian's freedom to enjoy a craft beer and a pipe. But Spurgeon's position was more complicated than that.

---

15 C.H. Spurgeon, *C.H. Spurgeon's Autobiography: Compiled from His Diary, Letters, and Records, by His Wife, and His Private Secretary.* Vol. 4 (London: Passmore & Alabaster, 1900), 128-129.

16 C.H. Spurgeon, ed. *The Sword and the Trowel; A Record of Combat with Sin & Labour for the Lord,* Vol. 18 (London: Passmore & Alabaster, 1883), 203.

17 C.H. Spurgeon, *The Metropolitan Tabernacle Pulpit: Sermons Preached and Revised by C. H. Spurgeon.* Vol. 42 (Pasadena, TX: Pilgrim Publications, 1970-2006), 177.

Spurgeon despised drunkenness and saw it as deadly sin that brought suffering in this life and sent people to hell in the next. He did not downplay its seriousness but urged all Christians to take action against it. At the same time, Spurgeon understood that Christians could have different ideas about the best way to deal with it. Christian liberty meant the freedom to hold to different positions on that issue. Both as one who drank in moderation, and later as a teetotaler, he urged both sides not to be quarrelsome or divisive in their position but to work together.

Additionally, as a pastor, Spurgeon knew he had a particular responsibility to his own congregation. In his preaching, he was concerned not to bind the consciences of his people beyond what was written in Scripture. He held the line of freedom during the smoking controversy, even though he found himself attacked on all sides. And once he became a teetotaler himself, he still maintained the primacy of the gospel. Teetotalism became an evangelistic tool, as he sought to bring those enslaved to drink to the One who could set them free.

But beyond these principles, this story also reveals something of Spurgeon's humanity. His inability to keep his early teetotaling commitments is striking, especially given how disciplined and competent he was in every other area of his life. He was not always careful in his speech and had to apologize for his comment about smoking to the glory of God. After decades of smoking, there likely was a level of dependence, even addiction, to tobacco, making it necessary for him to relax and sleep.[18] And in the end, his poor health likely did factor into his decision to be a teetotaler.

As we see in Romans 14 and 1 Corinthians 10, the discussion of Christian liberty arises in the context of some who are weaker in faith and others who are stronger. Spurgeon's convictions about temperance did not arise simply out of his ideals but were mixed with his struggles. Unlike Pentecost, who claimed to be delivered from his "pernicious habit" overnight, Spurgeon was never able to give up smoking. In his fight for Christian liberty, Spurgeon made room in the church not only for the strong, but also for the weak, including himself. Whether he was moderate or strict in his position, Spurgeon never lost sight of the importance of defending the liberty of conscience for all Christians.

---

18 When Fulton shared with Spurgeon that he had quit smoking, Spurgeon asked him, "Have you lost the appetite?... How do you get help when overcome with fatigue?" Fulton, *Spurgeon Our Ally,* 267. It appears by "appetite," Spurgeon is likely referring to his own dependence on smoking. Part of this was caused by his overwork and his need for a cigar to calm his nerves. On another occasion, Spurgeon declared, "When I have found intense pain relieved, a weary brain soothed and calm, refreshing sleep obtained by a cigar I have felt grateful to God, and have blessed His name." Spurgeon, . *The Metropolitan Tabernacle Pulpit: Sermons,* Vol. 42, 347.

Liberty of Conscience Requires Guardrails: Three Chapters of the Second London Confession

J. Ryan Davidson, ThM

Recently, in teaching my oldest child to drive, it was clear that the lines and lanes on the roadways before us were key for experiencing freedom on the road while driving. Lines and guardrails provide a freedom for us that would not be found should everyone have freedom or liberty to drive however they like. However, this reality sometimes seems counterintuitive. At the most basic level, how do boundaries actually make us more free? In the end, the answer of course is that they protect us, they provide a space for us to have liberty that is guided and safe, and they grant us a structure upon which we can travel down the road making decisions of liberty about our journey.

The Second London Confession (1677/1689) devotes and entire chapter to "Of Christian Liberty and Liberty of Conscience." However, that chapter comes in between two chapters which color the guardrails of such a chapter on Christian liberty. Specifically, Chapter 19 details a theology of the moral law of God, and Chapter 22 details Religious Worship and the Sabbath day. This brief article will sketch the connections between these three chapters and show that the theological truths of the law of God and of the Regulative Principle of Worship provide the boundaries for the road of Christian liberty.

The Second London Confession (1677/1689), chapter on Christian liberty begins in the following way:

> The liberty which Christ hath purchased for believers under the gospel, consists in their freedom from the guilt of sin, the condemning wrath of God, the rigour and curse of the law, and in their being delivered from this present evil world, bondage to Satan, and dominion of sin, from the evil of afflictions, the fear and sting of death, the victory of the grave, and everlasting damnation: as also in their free access to God, and their yielding obedience unto Him, not out of slavish fear, but a child-like love and willing mind...(2LCF 21.1)

Believers have been given a great gift of freedom in the Lord Jesus Christ. The Confession notes the glorious realities of this freedom. However, it is quick to point out the biblical reality that this Christian liberty is guarded by the call to not use this liberty to sin (to transgress the moral law of God, or any positive laws instituted in the New Covenant).[1] Baptist historian James Renihan helpfully points out that the Confession is written in such a way that each section depends on what has come in previous chapters, and informs what comes in subsequent chapters.[2] This reality is clearly seen in the connection of these three chapters. The chapter on liberty of conscience, for instance, depends on that liberty not being used as a "pretence" to practice sin, and this requires a clear definition of sin, which is provided in a previous section on the law of God. Chad Van Dixhoorn helpfully describes this when he writes, "The idea of Christian liberty is not that we are free to do or say or think whatever we can persuade our weak consciences to accept. On the contrary, one purpose of Christian liberty is to be freed from the power of sin itself...[3] Additionally, the section in the Second London Confession on Christian liberty also informs the later chapter on worship in a unique way.

While unveiling the biblical doctrine of Christian liberty, the Confession states (following the paragraph giving an introductory definition) that:

> God alone is Lord of the conscience, and hath left it free from the doctrines and commandments of men which are in any thing contrary to his word, or not contained in it. So that to believe such doctrines, or obey such commands out of conscience, is to betray true liberty of conscience; and the requiring of an implicit faith, an absolute and blind obedience, is to destroy liberty of conscience and reason also.

Given that the law of God has been clearly described in Chapter 19, now in Chapter 21 what is clear is that no one should be able to bind the conscience to things that the Lord has not commanded in his Word. The law of God then provides a guardrail on one side of Christian Liberty.[4] Liberty extends to the edge of the road where the law of God shows the boundary. However, as a Reformation-era document, the writers of the Confession wanted to address a specific topic where clear direction and prescription were being given to believers.[5] This was the area of gathered worship. It could be argued that gathered worship was a centerpiece of Puritan-era reforms. If life was

---

1   2LCF 21.3a "They who upon pretence of Christian liberty do practice any sin, or cherish any sinful lust, as they do thereby pervert the main design of the grace of the gospel to their own destruction, so they wholly destroy the end of Christian liberty..."

2   James M. Renihan, *A Toolkit for Confessions: Helps for the Study of English Puritan Confessions of Faith* (Palmdale, CA: Reformed Baptist Academic Press, 2017), 64.

3   Chad Van Dixhoorn, *Confessing the Faith: A Reader's Guide to the Westminster Confession of Faith*, (Carlisle, PA: Banner of Truth, 2014), 267.

4   The moral law of God is summarized in the Decalogue of the Old Testament and expounded upon in the Sermon of the Mount by the Lord Christ.

5   The Puritan John Owen has a helpful summary of related matters. See: John Owen, *Works*, (Edinburgh: Banner of Truth, Reprint 1965), 400–404.

to be lived in the world according to the moral law of God, and not by the dictates of men, then life within the gathered body of worship was also to be lived according to the commands of God.[6] In both cases, what drives the actions of believers are the commands of God—the lanes on either side of the road of Christian Liberty.

Notice how the introductory paragraph on worship in the Confession reads:

> The light of nature shews that there is a God, who hath lordship and sovereignty over all; is just, good and doth good unto all; and is therefore to be feared, loved, praised, called upon, trusted in, and served, with all the heart and all the soul, and with all the might. But the acceptable way of worshipping the true God, is instituted by himself, and so limited by his own revealed will, that he may not be worshipped according to the imagination and devices of men, nor the suggestions of Satan, under any visible representations, or any other way not prescribed in the Holy Scriptures.

Clearly seen here is what I previously mentioned: worship is "instituted by Himself [God]" and, similar to the verbiage of the chapter on Christian liberty which directly precedes it, it is stated that worship is free from the "imagination and devices of men."[7] Here we find the other lane that provides the freedom of the Christian liberty road. The Christian is truly free in worship when he or she is not commanded to do things that are not prescribed in the Scriptures. In fact, should a church not practice the regulative principle of worship (the understanding that public worship must involve only those things prescribed in the Word of God), then the conscience of the worshiper would be bound by the dictates and practices of other men.

Much like finding true freedom on the road in the lanes, Christian liberty is truly a reality when the lines of the moral law of God for life in the world and the regulative principle of worship for life among the gathered saintsare drawn on the road of our journey.[8] Without these two elements, there is no true Christian liberty, but rather, antinomianism along with the binding of the conscience of the Christian worshiper. One brilliant aspect of

---

6   It is helpful to have a clear distinction between moral law and positive law. Moral law is the eternal, abiding law of God for all times and all peoples which is a reflection of the nature of God. Positive laws are any commands that God gives under various periods of time, or covenants, which may pass away with those particular covenants or periods of time (i.e. Old Testament ceremonial laws of worship are positive, and are replaced with new positive laws under the New Covenant).

7   The Reformation-era issues within Puritan England are beyond the scope of this brief article. Nonetheless, they are clear contextual backgrounds to the statements found herein.

8   The Reformers and Puritans in general grounded the so-called "Regulative Principle of Worship" on the Second Commandment of the Decalogue.

the Confession (2LCF) is that it rightly teaches all three doctrines are crucial: the law of God, Christian liberty/freedom of conscience, and the regulative principle of worship. In doing so, there is true liberty for the follower of Christ.

American Slavery: A Tale of Two Evangelicalisms

Compiled, edited, and Introduced by Jordan A. Senécal

1. Introduction

In the antebellum years, a letter was written by the pen of Jean-Henri Merle d'Aubigné (1794–1872)—Merle, for short—a Genevan-born descendant of the Huguenots who served as a Protestant minister and professor in that city, as well as a key leader in the evangelical revival which swept across the French European landscape at the time known as *le Réveil*. Though Merle is the author of the letter, he wrote on behalf of dozens of ministers and professors who were involved primarily in the *Société évangélique de Genève* (the Evangelical Society of Geneva) and the *Église évangélique libre* (the Evangelical Free Church). The names of these men appear at the end of the letter, demonstrating their approval of what was written.

This letter, written in 1857, was sent to a minister in New York named Joseph Parrish Thompson (1819–1879), in order that he may disseminate it to be published in as many American publications and periodicals as possible. This letter serves as a worthy example of brotherly admonishment and seeking to offer correction in a spirit of humility and gentleness.

However, the letter was not well-received by all, and a rather scathing response was written and published in the *New York Daily Times* (now called the New York Times). The authors of the response are unknown, though they are presumably Christians, if not also Evangelicals.

Below I have included transcriptions of both the original letter sent by the Genevan Evangelicals and the response. I include these transcriptions not so much because they necessarily contain the strongest arguments made on either side of the debate, nor because they are both commendable, but they are a fascinating piece of history that still has ramifications down to this day. Be they what they are, they are a fascinating glimpse into the antebellum tensions surrounding American slavery and the drastically different viewpoints adopted by those who called themselves Christians (and, perhaps, even Evangelicals).

The tension would ultimately result in a devastating civil war that had countryman fighting countryman, neighbor fighting neighbor, Christian fighting Christian. The precursors to such disagreement are seen in these letters, and I trust this (lengthy) essay will shed light on not only the situation in the United States (as seen in the response), but even more so, in the plea sent by brothers overseas, who saw the reality of American slavery to be a matter of great concern.

1.1 LETTER OF MERLE D'AUBIGNÉ, D.D.[1]

The following letter is from the pen of Rev. J. H. Merle d'Aubigné, D.D., of Geneva. But it is not only the voice of the historian of the Reformation—the Protestantism of Europe here speaks to the Protestantism of America from a revered seat of our common faith, in tones so conciliatory and Christlike, that the most sensitive can not take offense. Will not the reader prayerfully consider this appeal, and also bring it to the knowledge of the church with which he is connected?

To the Evangelical Christians of the United States of America

Dearly beloved brethren in Christ, our all-sufficient Saviour and common Head:

The Evangelical Christians of Geneva frequently return thanks to God for having, in the days of Calvin, kindled that torch in their city, whose salutary light has spread throughout Europe, and reached your far-distant shores. They also give thanks to the Lord, that in these latter days, when the word of truth is penetrating into all nations of the earth, He has placed a powerful focus in North-America; and has sent the children of God from your churches both to enlighten the ancient countries of the East, where the Apostles themselves preached the Gospel, and to bring many souls out of heathen darkness to the Lord and Saviour. The work of propagating Christianity in all the world, is, in our opinion, dear brethren, the principal vocation which has been allotted to you from on high. Thus every thing which can strengthen the hands of

---

1   Jean-Henri *Merle d'Aubigné, Letter of Merle d'Aubigné, D.D.,* 1857. In transcribing the two letters, I have made an effort to preserve as much of the original style and formatting as possible, without being too archaic.

American Christians is, we think, an advantage to the whole world; whilst any thing which would weaken them is a real loss, a matter of grief, not to you alone, but to us, and to all mankind.

Now, dear brethren, we desire to express to you a thought which often presses itself upon our hearts. We fear that the laws which establish and regulate Slavery in several of your States, are a source of weakness, not only in your own dear country, but to her legitimate influence over other nations. We know that there are Christians in the United States who possess slaves, and we would not offend them. "Honor all men," says the Scripture (1 Peter 2:17), and above all, we wish to do so "to them that have obtained a like precious faith with us" (2 Peter 1:1). "We would assure them we come not to speak with them as enemies, but as brethren. We do not claim the right of imposing our opinion with authority upon them;—the Pope of Rome alone believes that he has that power;—and we do not doubt that those among you who differ from us on this subject, are sincere and upright in their opinions. However, if we would speak in love, we must also speak in truth, and with that precious liberty, which belongs to Christians. We know, moreover, that the city of Calvin is an object of deep and brotherly sympathy in America. Your citizens who visit us, are continually giving us fresh proofs of this, and this circumstance excites a hope that our request will find some favor in your eyes. But, we repeat, we do not pretend to teach you, but to give you a cordial token of our brotherly love.

Beloved brethren, if it is true, not only that Slavery is established in several of your States, but that in many places it is unlawful to instruct the children of slaves, or even for the parents to attend public worship; if it is true that the ties of husband and wife, parent and child, are often violently severed; if it is true that the master acquires the property and possession of a woman as if she were his own wife; if other facts, which we prefer not to describe here, are true—we ask ourselves, and we would also ask you, if such laws are compatible with the eternal principles of Christianity, which we all are bound to obey?

We might doubtless bring forward other arguments. We might remind you that Slavery is contrary to natural rights, and that all men having freedom alike, none can be deprived of that liberty unless forfeited by some criminal act; that the rights of property in men and in things are widely different, and that no man is allowed to sell a human being as he would a material object. We might say, with Montesquieu, that Slavery is hurtful alike to the slave and to the master; to the master especially, because he acquires all sorts of vices with his slaves. He becomes proud, hasty, passionate, hard, voluptuous, cruel. We might add, with that illustrious author, that in every country, however severe the toil which society exacts, its fruits may be obtained from freemen, by encouraging them with rewards and privileges, adapting the labor to their strength, by bringing to their aid machinery which art invents, and which, we might add, art has invented abundantly since the days of that great writer. But we prefer waiving such material considerations, and dwelling upon our argument in a Christian point of view.

We acknowledge, dear brethren, that Slavery is not explicitly abolished in the New Testament. We see that Christian masters are not prohibited from having slaves (Col. 4:1; Eph. 6:9); and that slaves are exhorted to submission and fidelity (Eph. 6:5, 8; Col. 3:22, 25; Titus 3:9, 10; 1 Peter 2:5, 18). Yes, slaves ought to be obedient and faithful, and nothing should be said which could drive them to revolt; that is certain; and yet it is as certain that Slavery is opposed to the true spirit of Christianity.

There are many texts in the New Testament which make this plain. Does not St. Paul say to the Christian slave, that if he can *obtain his freedom*, he is to take advantage of it (1 Cor. 7:21)? "The Apostle thus demonstrates that liberty is not only good, but also more advantageous than slavery," says Calvin.[2] Is it not also evident that slaves who have become Christians, should be regarded by their masters as *brethren*, according to the Epistle to Philemon? Does not the same Apostle, in another place, say that before the Lord in heaven *the slave is as the free* (Eph. 6:9)? Do not the Scriptures elsewhere declare that the slave and the free share in the same blessings of God in Jesus Christ, the Father, Son and Holy Ghost, one God, blessed for ever? Is He not the true and living God of the black as well as of the white man? If the Eternal Son, who is God for ever and ever, became man, was it not for the Greek as well as the Jew, for the slave as well as the free? Does not the righteousness which was acquired on the cross by the atoning blood of the Lamb, cover the sins of the one as well as of the other? Does the Holy Spirit, which changes the hearts of all in whom he dwells into temples of the Holy Ghost, make any distinction of color? Ought we not to exclaim now with the primitive Christians: "By one Spirit are we all baptized into one body, whether we be bond or free" (1 Cor. 12:13)? "There is neither bond nor free, but Christ is all and in all" (Col. 3:11).

Such being the teaching of the Scriptures, do you not think with us, beloved brethren, that these principles suppress the spirit of Slavery, and only leave its name and appearance? Do you not believe that since God, our common Father, bestows the tender sympathies of his love equally upon the

---

2   Taken from Calvin's commentary on 1 Corinthians 7:21.

slave and the free, we their brethren can not refuse the precious boon of liberty to those who are deprived of it? If Christ has made them free, shall not we free them also? Christianity in general did not lay violent or imprudent hands on civil institutions, but spread its principles everywhere, and gave precepts to all men, the application of which was gradually to bring about the suppression of all abuses.

These considerations are important; but, we repeat, what particularly induces us to make an appeal to your consciences, is the system of laws, manifestly opposed to the precepts of Christianity, with which several of your States have been obliged to burden their legislation, in order to maintain Slavery in the midst of you. It is not necessary to enumerate these laws; we know them from official documents published in Europe, and which have caused both astonishment and grief to the friends of religion, morality, and liberty. We are aware these laws do not exist in a good many of your States; we know that, with the exception of one or two laws, legislation on Slavery is local, instituted in their sovereign power by those States alone which maintain Slavery. But that in no way prevents us from freely expressing the sentiments which animate us, either to just and moderate men, who doubtless are to be found in abundance in the Southern States, or to all the Christians of the American Union.

If we mistake not, there are three classes of opinions and of persons in the United States, as to the present subject; one is decidedly against Slavery, another is decidedly in its favor; but there is a medium class which hesitates; and we think the moment has arrived when all those who belong to that class ought to decide before God and their conscience, wisely, but with courage and firmness. Between Christianity on one side, and utilitarianism on the other, we do not think that Christians should hesitate.

The two great features which characterize the United States, and which form the essence of your people, are they not, honored friends—the Gospel and Liberty! And are you not called upon both to enjoy these two blessings for yourselves, and to testify to others bow happy are those nations who possess them, and thus to be the means of spreading them in the world? Now it is precisely the Gospel and Liberty which are implicated in this question. The maintenance of Slavery must hinder the growth of these two great principles. The most eminent writers have shown that if Slavery may be excused in despotic States, it is in conflict with the essence of democracy, and that if it is more or less natural amidst Mohammedans and Pagans, it is impossible to justify it amongst Christians, and above all amongst Protestants. Yes, it is now in your power, dear American friends, to render the most brilliant homage, the most signal service, to the cause of the Gospel of Protestantism and of true Liberty. Will you hesitate?

How often we have mourned to see Roman Catholics and partisans of arbitrary governments triumph in pointing to the existence of Slavery in the United States! How often have we been tempted to exclaim: "Tell it not in Gath, publish it not in the streets of Askelon, lest the daughters of the Philistines triumph" (2 Sam. 1:20).

Dear brethren, listen to these voices, which come from a far distant land at the foot of the Alps, from the city of the Reformation, and are raised in concert with those in France and other countries. We would entreat you by the most precious interests; in the name of the prosperity of the Union, of the peace, of the glory of your country; in the name of the cause of true liberty; and, above all, of the holy and great cause of Christianity;—to do all in your power, with an unflinching fidelity, to bring about the suppression of Slavery and the establishment of social liberty in your country. Let it be done with wisdom, with kindness, with justice, without disturbing the public peace, but, notwithstanding, as promptly and as universally as possible.

Should this step offend you, dear brethren, we pray you to forgive us. We conjure you to bear with us. We say with St. Paul to the Corinthians, "If we are foolish, it is for the love of you;" it is, we believe, for the glory of Jesus Christ; it is because we thought that God, in a special manner, had called us so to do.

We live in solemn times. A new era is dawning on this question, not only in your country but in the whole civilized world. Universal attention is aroused. Everywhere public opinion pronounces with decision on this subject. The time is certainly come when America must give satisfaction to the claims of Christianity. We know that it is not easy to find the means of attaining that end. There will be many shoals and difficulties; but we know that your people have more courage than any others to surmount all these obstacles, and that the Lord will give the victory to those who are on his side. Let nothing stop your progress; combat Slavery in the spirit of the Gospel, and not in a mere worldly spirit. Seek, above all, the means of attaining this excellent end in a spirit of prayer. Look to the Word of God, to the spirit of Christianity, to the requirements of morality and liberty, and to Jesus the Redeemer, and thus go forward in the Lord's name. May God be your strength in this great, salutary, just, and Christian work. Let us assure you that such shall be our constant prayer!

The grace of our Lord Jesus Christ be with you all, Amen![3]

American Slavery: A Vindication of Slavery. Answer to a Letter from Geneva, Addressed to the Evangelical Christians of the United States of America[4]

The historian of the Reformation, MERLE D'AUBIGNE, with forty-six others, Presidents, Professors and Members of the Evangelical Churches and other Societies in Geneva, Switzerland, addressed a letter, on the 31st of March, 1857, to the Evangelical Christians of the United States, on the subject of Slavery. It has been published and widely circulated. We propose to give it a respectful answer.

We begin by objecting to the whole purpose of the letter, independently of its argument, as unauthorized, injudicious, and productive of evil. The writers profess to be induced by zeal only in the cause of truth; by a desire to see the great American Republic relieved from every *impediment in diffusing religious truth among all nations*; by a conviction that Providence has *fixed a great focus of*

---

3   The names of the signatories are as follows: **Merle D'Aubigné**, D.D., Président de l'École de Théologie et Vice-Président de la Société Évangélique; **L. Gaussen**, D.D., Professeur de l'École de Théologie et Membre des Comités de la Soc. Évan.; **H. Laharpe**, Professeur de l'École de Théologie, et membre du Comité de la Société Évan.; **C. Malan**, D.D., Pasteur de l'Église tu Témoignage; **H. Tronchin**, Colonel fédéral et Président du Comité Italien. **Adrien Naville**, Président du Comité de l'Alliance Évangélique et du Comité d'Évangélisation de la Soc. Évan.; **Ls. Brocher**, Président du Presbytère de l'Église Évan.; **Dr. D'Espine**, Vice-Président du Presbytère de l'Église Évan.; **Dr. Lombard**, Vice-Président du Presbytère de l'Église Évan.; **Emile Demole**, Pasteur, Membre du Presbytère; **S. Pilet**, Professeur de l'École de Théologie et Pasteur de l'Église Évan.; **E. Binder**, Professeur de l'École Évan.; **A. Le Fort**, Trésorier de la Soc. Évan.; **Dr. Panchaud**, Membre du Comité de la Soc. Évan.; **C. Crémieux**, Président du Comité de Colportage de la Soc. Évan. et Ancien; **E. Cramer**, Membre du Comité de la Soc. Évan. et Diacre; **Wm. Turrenttini**, Membre du Comité de la Soc. Évan. et du Comité des Missions; **G. Naville**, Membre du Comité de la Soc. Évan.; **H. Serment**, Avocat, Membre du Comité de la Soc. Évan.; **Ch. Hahn**, Membre du Comité de la Soc. Évan.; **F. Cramer**, Membre du Comité de la Soc. Évan.; **E. Gautier**, Major fed. Membre du Comité de la Soc. Évan.; **Charles Barde**, Pasteur, Président du Comité des Missions; **H. Lasserre**, Secrétaire de la Soc. des Missions et Membre de la Soc. Évan.; **Coulin**, Pasteur, Membre du Comité des Missions; **Albert Freundler**, Ministre, Membre du Comité des Missions; **P. F. Andersen**, Pasteur de l'Église Luthérienne, et Membre du Comité des Missions; **D'Espine**, Père, Secrétaire de la Soc. Biblique de Genève; **Le Comte Agenor de Gasparin; Maximilien Perrot, Président du Comité de l'Union Chrétienne des Jeunes Gens; Ch. Galopin, Membre du Comité de l'Union Chrétienne; F. Bertholet**, Pasteur, Membre du Presbytère; **Emile Guers**, Pasteur, Membre du Presbytère; **Th. Lhuillier**, Pasteur, Membre du Presbytère; **Ch. Saladin**, Ancien, de l'Église Évangélique; **E. Bieler**, Ancien, de l'Église Évan.; **A. Loup**, Ancien, de l'Église Évan.; **T. A. Glardon**, Ancien, de l'Église Évan.; **H. Dansse**, Diacre, de l'Église Évan.; **M. Briquet**, Diacre, de l'Église Évan.; **T. L. Villibourg**, Diacre, de l'Église Évan.; **L. Zimmerli**, Diacre, de l'Église Évan.; **E. Martine**, Professeur; **Perceval de Loriol**, Membre du Comité de la Soc. Évan.; **Wm. Rey**, Membre du Comité de la Soc. Évan.; **Hi. Morret**, V. D. M.

4   "American Slavery: A Vindication of Slavery. Answer to a Letter from Geneva, Addressed to the Evangelical Christians of the United States of America," *New York Daily Times*, August 20, 1857. There were parts of this article that were difficult to read and/or decipher. Where the text was unclear and I had to make a guess, I placed my guess in square brackets (i.e., [letter]). Where I was unsure of my guess, I followed it with a question mark (i.e., [letter?]).

light in the United States. They wish to increase it. They fear that Slavery is *a cause of weakness and they are anxious to remove it.* The thought presses on their hearts. They invoke us *by the peace and glory of our country, by true liberty, and the cause of Christianity,* to bring about *a suppression of Slavery.* "They do not claim the right to impose opinions by authority—the Pope of Rome alone believes that he has that power." They would exercise the right only of Christian liberty, and send us their advice as a token of Christian love. They believe that those who differ from them in opinion on the subject at issue, are sincere and upright men. They do not wish to offend their brethren, but to do them good.

If everything claimed for the intention of the writers be freely and fully conceded, their proceeding will make no exception to the truth that goodness of intention alone, in any important action, is not enough. Its purity is no justification or excuse for interfering—we will not say intermeddling—in the affairs of a distant and independent community—still less, in a difficult and disputed question of social policy, which divides and inflames the minds of its people.

They address themselves to prejudiced and angry partizans. They letter is welcomed on the one side as a support; it is resented on the other as an attack. It is not sufficient to say that nothing of the sort is intended. We know it is not intended. But, we repeat, goodness of intentions is no defence for causing mischief. If it be the Christian's duty to do good, it is his duty to also refrain from the appearance of evil. If he must impart benefits, he must beware lest his benefits prove fire-brands of discord and death. To intervene in the affairs or disputes of others, promotes dissension, not peace. The maxim needs no illustration. It applies alike to individuals, families, societies and nations.

At all times, States and communities are the best judges of their own business. Neither governors nor counselors a long way off are safe and sufficient guides. Our whole American history is an assertion and vindication of this truth. No government abroad, proprietary or royal, satisfied our people. They never ceased to contend, until they had established the right to manage their affairs in their own way. Our country's great maxim is not to interfere with others, and not to permit interference with herself. This is the best security for peace among nations. Let the lovers of peace be cautious how they infringe the spirit of the rule in the least important particular.

But our friends of Geneva are not interfering as a State with a State; they intermeddle only as a Society of Christians with other Christian Societies. They are for that reason the more subject to the applications of the rule. If interference be indefensible, it is the more indefensible when forced or attempted by Christian communities, the advocates of forbearance and peace.

They are governed, as they think, by a principle of conscience. Alas, Christian friends! this opinion only increases the probability of mischief by concealing the danger. We never do evil, says the comparable PASCAL, so cheerfully and effectually as when we do it on a false principle of conscience. Can you be sure that your uninvited interference in the domestic policy of a distant people is resting on a true one? You believe that God has called you "in a special manner," to interpose on this occasion. Where is the evidence? You tell us that you will say to us, as St. Paul said to the Corinthians, in advising them, "If we are foolish, it is for the love of you." But St. Paul had charge of the Church at Corinth; he had proof of being called in a special manner. You have no charge in this matter, and no proof of a special calling. If, nevertheless, the Apostle apologised in advising, what shall we say of your venturing to do what he excused himself for doing?

You do not claim "the right to impose opinions by authority—the Pope alone believes that he has that power." Yet the Pope of Rome is silent when you assume to speak. You charge him with arrogating the power which you substantially though quietly exercise, but which, in this matter, he has never undertaken to assert.

You do not impose opinions—very true; but there is a small interval only between imposing opinions and imposing advice. How easy to pass from one to the other! The invitation of a monarch is a command. The counsel of authority implies submission. The temper that volunteers advice is the temper that exacts obedience. The power may be wanting, but not the will. The man who denounces one creed will enforce another by violent means. You who now volunteer to counsel on our principles and practice, under different circumstances from similar views with equal intentions, would compel obedience to what you believe to be the will of God and the good of the Church. Is there no lamentable fact in the history of Geneve itself which may serve, in reference to this truth, as an illustration and warning?

It is the duty of Christians, you think, to feel a warm sympathy in the condition and character of other Christians: to be active in giving effect to their sympathy; to be ready not only with their prayers but with counsel and other aid. All this is true, but all within just limits only. They may advise, but the advice must be sought; it must be founded on a thorough knowledge of the facts; of the temper of the party advised; of the limits of his means and power to act; of the effects direct and indirect of the measure suggested for adoption. Do you stand within these limits? Have you the necessary knowledge for judicious counsel? You say to us if your custom is this, if your practice is that—*if the slave is not allowed by law to attend public worship; if* it is *unlawful to instruct the children of slaves;* "*if* the master acquires possession of a woman as *if* she were his own wife;" if these and other facts are true, can your laws, you ask us, be compatible with the eternal principles of Christianity? You thus grope about, on hands and knees, to seek what ground you stand upon, or whether you stand on any. You go on blindly to give counsel as though your *ifs* were facts, while, in truth, they are slanders only, on your American brethren. Are they not founded on hearsay, on the inventions of a fictitious story? We greatly fear that you have no better authority for your opinions than the incidents of a popular tale. Have you been cautious and considerate in this matter? Have you borne in mind the proneness that besets us all to assume the office of supervising our brother's affairs and teaching him his duties—the ease with which we decide what it becomes others to do or bear, or suffer; the equanimity with which we support another's pains or losses; the generosity with which we do liberal deeds at another's cost—have these things been sufficiently before your eyes?

You admit that there are, in the Southern States of North America, "just and moderate men in abundance." There is more than this. There are well educated, wise, devout and holy men, laborious teachers and ministers of Christian truth, men who traverse interminable forests, crossing mighty rivers, braving the malaria of deadly regions, not unworthy followers and fellow-laborers of the great Apostle of the Gentiles, in deaths often, in perils of the wilderness, in hunger, in cold, in nakedness, perseveringly and successfully preaching the whole gospel of Christ. Are you acquainted, as they are, with the negro character—his need of subjection, his inability to sustain any competition with the white man, his dullness, his idleness, his improvidence? It is easy to say that all this is the delusion of the slaveholder. But can you know it to be so? What are your opportunities for knowing? You make no investigation. You take the opinions of those ready like yourselves to interfere without knowledge. Is this Christianity humility or candor, or just respect for the character of Christian men, as wise and good as yourselves, and infinitely better informed on the question which you undertake to decide? Never has there been a stronger illustration of the truth that it is a small thing to be judged of man's judgment. Who are ye that judge these devout and laborious men? Have you stood face to face as they do, with the social condition of which you speak? Have you searched it as they search it? Can you understand it as they do? Have you been engaged, as slaveholding Christians have been for a century, in caring for the negro race, in feeding, clothing, training to useful labor, restraining, instructing, civilizing, Christianizing the African? The Christian masters and ministers of the Southern States have done and are doing all this. What have you done? What labors have you performed? What sacrifice have you made? By what right do you assume that you are the negro's friend, and his master's too? Let us be understood—we make no boast, we claim no merit. We have done only what Providence appointed us to do—very imperfectly, it may be, without sufficient devotion to the divine will of which are instruments and agents! But all that has been done, the Slaveholders have done. It has been done with immense benefit to the African race. Where else do you find them, as you find them here, efficient laborers, living in peace, bestowing blessings on the whole world, civilized men, compared with the natives of Africa? Who supplies your manufactories with cotton? Who furnishes your laborers the soothing influences of their indispensable narcotic? Who produces the sugar and rice that add to your comforts and luxuries? Is it the African in Africa? Do you obtain these great commercial products from Guinea and Angola? And where else, except among the slaves of the Southern States of American, are seen, in hundreds of thousands, negroes composing Christian Churches in whole or in part? Where else will you find multitudes of negroes able to read the Gospel? In what other region has the African increased, in a century, from 300,000 to 300,000,000? And now when the negro has been converted from a savage to a man, to a prosperous and intelligent peasant, artisan and Christian, by those who have lived with him, and guided and governed him, you stand afar off, and undertake to reprove their remissness, and direct their proceedings. You call across the Atlantic to the laborers in this remote Christian vineyard, who are diligently and faithfully preaching and teaching, by precept, and example, every moral and religious duty, and administering from day to day the Christian sacraments to thousands of churches composed of Christian negroes, and you say to them, my Christian brethren, *if your slaves are not allowed to attend on public worship, if you never teach them, if you have as many wives as you have negro women slaves,* we exhort you to hear our counsel, offered with Christian liberty, in Christian love.

As it has been the lot of the Christian slaveholder to do all that has been done, it will be for him and him alone to do all that is to be done for the negro race in North America. It is not the task of a day, or a century, to change a barbarous to a civilized race. It needs time, patience, perseverance. The present civilization of Europe is the work of more than two thousand years. You are impatient; you would anticipate the labor of ages—you who have no portion in the toil, no part of the responsibility, no share in the risk arising from injudicious or hurried proceedings—you are unwilling to leave the business to Providence and to the agencies chosen for it by Providence. We are as willing to do what is right as you are; we alone are able to do anything in this matter; we ask you, with all Christian frankness, to stand aside and let us do the work. It is ours, not yours. You may embarrass, but you cannot help us. You may trouble us, but you cannot share our task.

You advise us to abolish Slavery—are you prepared to offer us a plan for effecting it with safety and advantage to all parties? The physician who is content to tell his patients that they are sick and suggests no practicable cure, or who prescribes medicine and knows nothing of its virtues, will command no confidence in his skill. You tell us we are suffering under an evil; you call upon us to remove it; can you devise any mode of doing so with that regard for the general safety which ought, you think, to be carefully considered? What is to be done with the blacks when manumitted? The race, although improved in North America, is still a barbarous one. They are sluggish and sensual. They are inferior to the white not only in actual progress, but in ability to advance. They cannot, like the freed men of Greece or Rome, melt into the mass of freemen. People of the same type, English and Irish, German and French, are easily moulded into one American mass, but there is no possible compounding of white and black. This may seem very unreasonable and wrong to you who know nothing of the difficulty, but it is not the less true. If the two races remain together in the same country, the destruction of the inferior becomes inevitable. We ask you to be taught by history. The great tribes of red men who formerly inhabited North America, have all perished from between the Mississippi and the ocean. The black millions would be equally unfortunate if removed from the control and care of the white race. They could not sustain a competition for bread with a more intelligent rival. This is seen to be true in Canada and in the Northern States. From this cause, with no wars to precipitate it, the extirpation of the blacks must follow manumission. Even where climate protects him from white competition and its consequences, the black deteriorates in freedom. Eye witnesses in the English West India Possessions declare that he is more idle, vicious and ignorant than when a slave. His progress in civilization seems to be conditional on his subjections to a more intelligent and energetic people. Suppose, then, that as the necessary consequence of manumission, the black race should waste away and perish; or, that they should become more idle, vicious, improvident and miserable. What then? Will you still say to us manumit your slaves? Will you disorganize the labor of a whole country, endanger its existence, destroy its great commercial products so important to the whole world, with the certainty of ruin to the race you desire to benefit? Will you convert three millions of useful laborers into paupers and thieves that could not remain in their present home, and that would not find homes anywhere else? We are afraid that you have never given a thought to the subject. If you have, propose to us your plan.

In the early history of the Church, we can find no examples of one society of Christians interposing with unasked advice, or instruction, or otherwise, in the affairs of another. We see but one in which there was any interference at all. When certain parties from the hill country of Judea troubled the Gentile converts with unauthorized teachings and advisings, seeking to impose as Christian duties what were none, an appeal was made to the Apostles and Elders at Jerusalem—to the inspired teachers of Christianity. The men who troubled the Churches were rebuked. The Council, under the immediate influence of the Holy Spirit, advised or admonished the Churches. Do you hold the same authority as the Apostles? Have you been called upon in like manner to advise? Can you claim the same special guidance of the Holy Spirit? Or are you not rather in the position of the parties against whom the Council was called and the decision was made? We fear so. You have troubled Christian Societies with teachings not in Scripture. You have attempted to impose on them as Christian duties what they deny to be such. It was the duty of circumcision formerly. It is the duty of abolishing Slavery now. There are no living inspired Apostles; we must turn, therefore, to their writings. Show us in these writings the Apostle's precept—manumit your slaves. It would be as easy to find one commanding Christians to circumcise their children. You are teaching without authority what the Apostles have not taught; you are giving counsel where it has not been invited; you interfere in the social condition of a remote community where you may do harm to the cause of Christ, but can do no good.

We make these remarks in not captious or unkind spirit. But the surest way to promote the brotherly intercourse of Christian Churches and communities is to restrict it within safe and legitimate limits. Even between friend and friend, advice, if unasked, if unseasonable, or unfounded on sufficient knowledge of the facts of the case and the feelings of the parties, is always injudicious, seldom useful, often mischievous. It has already produced the worst consequences among our American Churches. The intervention of those abroad can only increase the mischief. There are now divisions and dissentions arising from the attempt of some to assume control over the consciences of others. You may increase the evil by interposing; you cannot remove or lessen it.

And here, with a protest against the whole form and purpose of the letter from Geneva, we might close our answer or review. But we are reluctant to seem wanting in respect for the authors and their arguments, or unwilling to give them our most serious attention. We will, therefore, proceed to examine the reasons against Slavery which they are pleased to assign.

They begin with arguments of more general consideration, but rely on such as apply peculiarly to Christian men. "We might remind you," they say, "that Slavery is contrary to natural rights; that all men having freedom alike, cannot be deprived of that liberty unless forfeited by some criminal act; that the right of property in men and things is widely different; that no man is allowed to sell a human being as he would a material thing." And they quote the remarks of MONTESQUIEU as to the injurious effects of Slavery on both master and slave. To such remarks it is enough to say that Slavery is not a new thing under the sun. It has existed in all ages of the world, and its injurious effects, whatever they may be, have not prevented the masters of slaves from being the most renowned warriors, the most eloquent orators, judicious historians and profound philosophers, the most accomplished poets, painters, sculptors, or architects that the world has ever seen.

Nothing, Christian friends, can be more delusive and dangerous in practical questions than conclusion drawn from theories of natural rights. The French Revolution was a grand drama, arranged to illustrate and enforce this important truth. It overturned all social, civil and political relations. It decreed an end to religion. It was the first to abolish negro Slavery. The present abolition spirit is the legitimate offspring of the school of liberty, equality, fraternity, whose doctors and apostles were GREGORIE, BRISSOT, ROBESPIERRE, and whose legitimate effects were brutal massacres, at which the world still stands aghast. We detest them and all their [cant?]. There is no state of nature. It is unknown even among the most barbarous tribes. Men exist in societies only. They are born into certain conditions, subject to certain restraints and penalties, imposed by governments over which they have no control. Their rights are determined by laws, and laws are what the good of society requires them to be. Whatever this may demand, society has the right to enact. You admit that a man may be deprived of his freedom for a criminal offence. Why so? Why should the law deprive a felon of his freedom? It may do more, it may take his life. If society can take life to secure what it deems the good of society, will it be pretended that it cannot for the same reason compel its members to serve it as slaves? If the reason is sufficient to imprison or hang one man, is it not enough to enslave another? We say nothing of the looseness of thorough or language by which you confound the condition of the prisoner and the slave; and regard them as deprived of liberty in the same sense. But supposing that they are, what right has the State in the case of the criminal that it has not in an equal degree in that of the slave? If the good of society does not require the enslaving a part of its population or the imprisonment of the criminal, it is wrong to enslave or imprison; if it does require them, it is right. In either case, the discretion of society must of necessity be the measure of the right. It has been exercised accordingly in all ages, by all States, and when it is said that a man cannot be deprived of his freedom, except for a criminal offence, the assertion is made in defiance of the codes of all nations, beginning with that of the great legislator and prophet of Judea. It is in vain to any, in the face of all example to the contrary, that the good of a State can never require the enslaving of a part of its people. This is simply assuming as true the whole question that you undertake to prove. It is making your judgment the standard of right; it is asserting what you disdain—the power to impose opinions by authority. Others have attempted to prove that the good of society never requires the gibbet or the jail; that criminals should not be deprived of life or freedom; that education only should be opposed to crime. They may with equal reason demand that their dogmas should be assumed as truth.

The Southern States of North America judge it to be essential to their welfare that the negro portion of their population should be slaves. They exercise the right of all States to determine what is essential to their own welfare. They injure no other State. They affirm no universal propositions or abstract questions in relation to Slavery as a general question, or as concerning other States. They are no propagandists. They confine their views to the practical question only that concerns themselves. They claim to be allowed to exercise their discretion in their own affairs. Surely, Christian friends, there is reason in this.

The right of property, you say, in men and things is widely different—certainly it is. We never said or thought otherwise. You have formed false conceptions of Slavery, and oppose imaginary principles and maxims, never maintained among us. No man, you add, is allowed to sell a human being as a material thing—very true; and no master of slaves ever sells a human being as a material thing. What is sold and what is bought, in every sale of slaves, is the labor only of the slave, coupled with the obligation to support him. What is there so monstrous in this? Suppose a peasant, bound for life to one of your farmers, with the power in the farmer to transfer the laborer to another farmer, each successive employer being obliged to support the peasant and his family, would this be an insupportable evil to the peasant? Would it place him in any greatly worse condition than he now holds, with an equal obligation to labor and the uncertainty of obtaining work? Would it make him a material thing? Substitute in the case supposed the word slave for peasant and master for farmer, and you will understand the real condition of Negro Slavery in the United States. Emancipate yourselves from the dominion of words. The slaveholder does not sell the negro's body and soul, as certain pestilent declaimers tell you. He claims and sells nothing but the negro's labor. He has in the slave for life no more than your farmer has in his ploughman or reaper for a day, or a month, or a year. It is only a different system of labor from your system. Yours is best for your peasantry, no doubt, but we have as little doubt that ours is best for the negro. The slave with us is bound to labor—that is the phrase of the Federal Constitution—as the apprentice is bound to labor with you; the one for life, the other for a limited period. The selling of the one as little implies that he is considered a material thing, as the apprenticing of the other. If you ask who binds the slave and makes him an apprentice for life, we reply, the same power that binds the apprentice for a term of years—the laws of the land; and, for the same cause, too,—the inability of the parties to govern themselves.

Slavery is not the creature of the master's unrestrained will, nor is it left to his discretion. The master's obligations are determined by law—by lay sustained, and enforced by an active and sensitive public opinion. The master is the guardian of the slave, to protect him, to support him, not only in health and strength, but in old age and infancy. The instance is unknown in this country of a slave dying from want. He is undisturbed by taxes and conscriptions. His life is one of peaceful labor and certain subsistence. But of all this you know nothing. You never inquire, you only condemn. You join in the current clamor of the world in its denunciation of a system of which your best information is uncertain hearsay. There is as little philosophy as charity in this.

A thinking man might find something worthy of the most careful research in a domestic policy which is so connatural to mankind as to prevail at all times with all varieties of people—with the strong practical sense of the Roman, the refined intellect of the Greek, the deep religious sentiment of the Hebrew. Serfage, villeinage, feudalism, slavery, are all modifications only of the principle which subjects the weak to the strong, the inferior to the superior, for the benefit of both, but especially of the feebler party. The universality of the policy shows its inherency in our nature. It springs up in society in certain stages, under certain circumstances, as certainly as trees in a forest, and is as native to human necessities as grass to the fields. It disappears before advancing civilization, under other circumstances, as the wood disappear before increasing cultivation. In either case the result is the work of causes that we can neither hasten nor retard. We have no space, however, for inquiries like these, and leave to your reflections.

But you do not insist on these material considerations. You prefer to waive them. You desire to dwell on the argument in a Christian point of view. In this view of it you say, "We acknowledge, dear brethren, that Slavery is not explicitly abolished in the New Testament; we see that masters are not prohibited from owning slaves; that slaves are exhorted to submission and fidelity—that is certain; and *yet it is as certain* that Slavery is opposed to the spirit of Christianity."

But if Slavery is opposed to the true spirit of Christianity, it is, above all doubt, certain that the Apostle has said so—that he has clearly and emphatically instructed or advised Christian masters to manumit their slaves. We defy any human ingenuity to escape from the absolute necessity of this conclusion. You feel the necessity—it is unavoidable—and while you admit that Slavery is not explicitly abolished in the New Testament, you adduce passages in which you think the Apostle has plainly taught Christians that Slavery is inconsistent with the spirit of Christianity. We believe that the passages bear no such interpretation.

The first quoted is from 1 Corinthians, vii. 21. The quotation is confined to part of the verse included in the parenthesis below. To understand it we must read the preceding and succeeding verses. "Let every one," the Apostle says, "remain in the station in which he has been called to be a Christian; art thou called being a slave, care not for it, *(but if thou mayest be free use it rather;)* for he that is called in the Lord being a slave is the freeman of the Lord; likewise also, he that is called being free is the slave of the Lord." The whole scope of the passage is to inculcate by the most emphatic language that it is unimportant in the eyes of God what the condition of life may be, in which a Christian is placed. Let each remain in his station. Be content with your condition; do its duties faithfully; that only is important. The Lord is no respecter of person. All are alike to him, wise or simple, prince or peasant, bond or free. Yet in the midst of this most emphatic declaration that it is not important what a Christian's station may be, the Apostle turns aside, as you think, to teach the slave that it is important. The Apostle, as you represent him, is very much in the position of an actor who declaims one sentiment aloud to the audience, and, in a stage whisper, aside, to a different party, expresses another. The passage of Scripture in its whole scope says one thing; and you make a parenthesis of half a dozen words demonstrate the reverse. You are aware that a number of the ablest commentators, from Chrysostom to the present time, give the passage a meaning which, they say, the original demands, and which is the very opposite to your own. They construe the words in the parenthesis to this effect—if thou art a slave care not for it, *(and even if you may obtain freedom, remain, nevertheless, in your [station?].)* The interpretation is in harmony with the whole passage, and renders it more emphatic still. Yours contradicts and confuses it. There is yet another sense in which the words may be taken which we presume to suggest as the meaning of the Apostle. A Christian slave offered his freedom, might have been embarrassed, under the strong peremptory teaching of the Apostle, to decide whether he could, if he wished it, accept the offer or not. To relieve that embarrassment, the Apostle limits his precept and leaves the decision to the slave's discretion—if offered freedom, he says, you may accept it if you wish it; you will not in so doing disregard my precepts. This interpretation conforms to the general purpose of his instructions. But to represent him as engaged in demonstrating certain abstract propositions concerning Freedom or Slavery, is incompatible with his whole aim and meaning. He was giving practical rules for the regulation of life in every condition, not suggesting reasons for preferring one condition.

But if this parenthetical remark addressed to the slave is to be regarded as affirming that slavery is inconsistent with Christianity, something more decided still must be inculcated on the master by the Apostle. He has not preached to the slave, and been silent to the master in a matter that concerns them both. You must show us his injunction to masters. You are convinced that this is necessary, and accordingly you quote Ephes. i. 9: "Before the Lord in heaven the slave is as the free"; and 1 Cor. xii. 13: "We are baptized into one body whether we be bond or free"; and, lastly, Col. iii. 11: "There is neither bond or free, but Christ is all in all." These passages you adduce, to prove that the Apostle teaches the master that Slavery is inconsistent with the spirit of Christianity; and you go on to ask, whether God is not the God of the black man as well as the white man; whether the blood of the cross does not cover the sins of the one as well as the other; whether the Holy Spirit makes no distinction in spiritual things, between white or black, lord or laborer, prince or peasant, ruler or ruled, doctor or disciple; and lest Christians should be misled by this truth—as they have been often and greviously—to overturn all government, to abolish slavery, to level the condition of rule and ruled, prince and peasant, doctor and disciple, he enjoins on them with repeated, emphatic, peremptory earnestness to remain content with their conditions, to submit to rulers, to obey masters, for distinction in temporal things are made by providence—the powers that be are ordained of God.

But assuredly if the Apostle had intended to teach the Christian Church that Slavery is inconsistent with "the eternal principles of Christianity," he would not have been content with hinting this truth indirectly and obscurely, and leaving to modern believers to supply his imperfect doctrine. Was he slack, or careless, or timid, or time-serving in preaching the Gospel? Woe is unto me, he says, if I preach not the Gospel. Was he indirect, whose peculiar excellence it was to be plain and straightforward; and not as one beating the air. Was he fearful of consequences, who traveled through perils and sufferings innumerable to final martyrdom? Was he backward to incur responsibility, who condemned every sin and social evil, who omitted to notice no abuse even in dress or manners? If Slavery is what you represent it to be, an offence among Christians not to be told in Gath nor published in the streets of Ascalon [i.e., Ashkelon], it is as certain as truth, that the Apostle has explicitly denounced it. He has not been content with a side-wind condemnation of it. It was part of the gospel ministry to reprove it. If he neglected to reprove it openly and fearlessly, he has incurred the woe which he invoked on himself, if he preached not the gospel. He has the subject repeatedly before him. He enjoined on masters their duties to their slaves. And yet, you say, he omitted the most important of them all. Either the Apostle shrunk from his duty, or you, my good friends, are mistaken in yours.

You feel this difficulty. It is indeed not to be escaped. Therefore, to meet it, you say, "Christianity did not lay violent or imprudent hands on civil institutions." This is the reason assigned why the Apostle has not performed the duty which you are now performing for him. But, to enjoin masters to manumit their slaves, would in no wise have laid violent hands on civil institutions. It was no infringement of civil institutions in the Roman Empire to manumit a slave. Nothing was more common. The Apostle would have affronted no law, custom or prejudice, by enjoining it. He might have said to his converts, manumit your slaves as heathen masters continually manumit theirs. It is of daily occurrence among them. Do not allow their benevolence to exceed yours. Was it assailing the civil institutions to advise Christians to do what all the world were doing? It was more easy to manumit the slave then than now. The slave of Greek, Roman or Hebrew, was of no inferior race. The freedman easily amalgamated with the mass of freemen. The slave was often the equal of his master in learning, accomplishments and manners. A [generation?] removed all distinctions. There was no insuperable barrier of color or inferior capacity. There was no question then, as now, what is to become of the manumitted slaves.

But if to manumit a slave was to lay violent hands on civil institutions, the Apostle nevertheless, as we believe, would not have hesitated to enjoin the manumission of slaves, had he believed Slavery to be inconsistent with the spirit of Christianity. He would have reproved it with as little scruple as he reproved the worship of idols. Idolatry made a part of the civil government. To refuse attendance in the national temples was an offence to the laws. Did the Apostle hesitate to denounce idolatry? We are commanded to render unto CÆSAR the things that are CÆSAR's—tribute to whom tribute is due. But it is not due to CÆSAR to commit sin. In forbearing to reprove it, through his whole ministry, the Apostle was grievously neglecting his duty. But he could not have disregarded the duties of his ministry or failed in fighting the good fight to which he had devoted his whole life. The only alternative conclusion is, that the opinion which makes Slavery inconsistent with the spirit of Christianity is a dogma of modern invention, and a corruption of Christian doctrine. It is false, or the Apostles were unfaithful.

You say that the Apostles did not lay imprudent hands on civil institutions, but gave precepts that would bring about the suppression of all abuses, and you intimate that for this cause they laid no injunction on masters to manumit their slaves. Why then have you not followed the apostle's example? His silence is full of meaning. It means that his disciples are not to say what he refrained from saying. In teaching what he has not taught, are you not incurring the anathema of those who preach any other gospel than he preached? Why do you advise where he forbore? If to advise manumission is laying violent hands on civil institutions, why do you lay violent hands on civil institutions—on those, too, of a distant people with whom you have no immediate concern? Are you not doing more? Are you not laying imprudent hands on the ordering of God's Providence? Is it not probable, fellow Christians, that God's overruling will has brought to North America these millions of Africans for some good purpose? May you not safely trust the event to his wisdom and to the precepts that you say are to bring about the suppression of all abuses? Will your interference quicken their operation or give shape to God's purposes? When you go a long way off to do the work of others, may you not be neglecting your own? We think this consideration has some weight and is entitled to your serious consideration.

Would it not be wiser than to leave this whole serial question of negro slavery in North America to those who are most deeply concerned, to whom Providence has assigned it, who know it best, who are, in all respects, [...?] than you can be, for [meeting?] [...?] difficulties? Your American brethren, we venture to assure you, are as sincere Christians, as anxious to perform their duty, as quick to see it, as those who have given them counsel. We say it with no lack of respect, or kindness, or just appreciation of the friendly intentions that have produced your letter. But we fear, nevertheless, that you have only added another illustration to the truth of the admonitory phrase, *"ne accesseris in consilium antequam voceris."*[5]

---

5   "Do not come to the assembly until you are summoned."

Book Review:
The Making of Biblical Womanhood

Barr, Beth Allison. *The Making of Biblical Womanhood: How the Subjugation of Women Became Gospel Truth*. Grand Rapids: Brazos Press, 2021. 256pp. Softcover. ISBN: 9781587434709. $19.99.

Reviewed by Jordan L. Steffaniak, ThM

1. Introducing *The Making of Biblical Womanhood*

Discussion on topics related to gender and sexuality continue to provoke lively discussions and debates among evangelicals today. Beth Allison Barr's recent *The Making of Biblical Womanhood* is no different. The proof is easy to find. There is a slew of popular thinkers that praise her book ranging from Kristin Kobes Du Mez to Aimee Byrd to Jemar Tisby. As of the writing of this review, Barr's book is ranked #2 in Amazon's "Gender and Sexuality in Religious Studies" section and #11 in Amazon's "Christian Church History" section. But there are also several popular critical reviews of the book as well, including from *Themelios*. Suffice to say, Barr's book has been quite popular and has served as a lightning rod for some. If you aren't familiar with Barr, she is Professor of History and Associate Dean of Graduate Studies at Baylor University. She finished her PhD in 2004 at the University of North Carolina Chapel Hill with a research focus on women and gender identity in medieval and early modern English sermons. So, she is a well-trained and acclaimed historian. Add those credentials to a topic that is potent in contemporary theology, and you have a recipe for a wide readership and strong opinions.

Now, I don't normally review popular level books such as this one—especially those related to hot topics like gender. It's nearly impossible to please *anyone*. You'll be too harsh, too soft, too vague, or too squishy. So, I want to comment on *why* I've chosen to do so since I know such a review will likely please no one. In short, I love the pursuit of truth and the intellectual process that comes from thinking about big and important ideas. And understanding the role for women in the church of Christ is a big and important topic. So, from a purely abstract perspective, I'm always tempted to write a book review of *any* book because I think a well-done review has the ability to open up topics for readers (and myself as I re-read an author's work time and time again). It leads to new worlds, new ideas, and new ways to think about old topics. It removes poor arguments, poor ideas, poor ways to think about the world, and provides a window into a different way of being. Even when severe, reviews are ways of honoring authors and readers, charting a clearer path through the world of ideas. But enough about the virtues of a book review in general.

The reason I ended up deciding to read Barr's book and write a review is because I read Kevin DeYoung's negative review in *Themelios* several months ago and found it to be scathing if true. However, I had my own reservations that his review was sufficiently committed to charity. For example, I don't find appeals to "another side" of personal stories that DeYoung mentioned to be all that compelling or relevant for book reviews. Nor do I find stylistic grievances evidence to reject something in a book (DeYoung's laundry list of "historian" self-descriptors). And having given myself to reading a significant amount of literature (primarily philosophical, I'll confess!) on gender, I have a hard time trusting most evangelicals who discuss the issue on points besides basic exegesis of biblical texts. So, I was uneasy with his review. Of course, my uneasiness is not shared by most in my own confessional tribe, much to their chagrin. I'm more willing to hear another "side" than most. But I'm a philosopher. I like to hear alternative ideas and give them a fair shot—give me your best punch! But even with that in mind, I had intended to let this one go. The topic is just too volatile. But her book kept coming back up with claims of unfairness and uncharity. So, I decided to finally pick it up and read it for myself. I was surprised, to put it mildly. I found that I ended up agreeing with a significant portion of DeYoung's review. But I found several other serious deficiencies that DeYoung left untouched, or at least underdeveloped. Therefore, I think it's worthy to discuss them. However, in my own commitment to charity, I think there are points that ought to be considered by those like me who seek to hold firm to the historic confession of what is unsavory to many today—only men are to be ordained as elders.

Before I begin, I'll tell you my conclusion up front: Barr's book is riddled with serious deficiencies. While there are areas Barr has identified as problematic that *are problematic,* she does not fairly explain or resolve them. And while Barr's medieval historical expertise is fascinating and sorely needed, it does not cover for her faults. Therefore, while I have many egalitarian friends whom I greatly respect, have read many egalitarian works that I have benefited and learned from, *and* have no doubt the sincerity in Barr's thesis, I cannot recommend *this* book as a worthwhile companion. In fact, I think the faults in the book ought to lead *both* complementarians and egalitarians to find the book deeply wanting.

2. Summarizing *The Making of Biblical Womanhood*

Barr's main goal throughout her work is to show that the modern concept of "biblical womanhood" is just that—a modern construct devoid of biblical truth. It is a modernized version of "patriarchy." And the church continues a "long historical tradition of subordinating women" when it is patriarchal and bars women from preaching, leading, and teaching (20). Therefore, Barr argues that patriarchy is a part of the fall and that it isn't divinely ordained (25). Her work is framed by her own personal story of pain due to her and her husband's shifting view on women in ministry and her husband's resultant firing from their church, with snippets being presented throughout. Barr begins her work in chapter one by defining "patriarchy" in society at large and the Christian church. She claims that patriarchy is identical to *Christian* patriarchy (16–18). Patriarchy takes power from women and teaches that women are less important than men (18). Barr then argues that patriarchy originates with human civilization itself (35).

Chapter two attempts to re-examine the Apostle Paul and suggests that rather than restricting women, he does nothing of the sort—anyone who thinks otherwise is captive to modern cultural categories (41). Barr explains that the Pauline texts that are often used by evangelical Christians (think texts like 1 Tim. 2) are mysteriously absent from late medieval sermons. The difference between the two cultures is evidence that the texts have been grossly misunderstood by modern Christians. Take the household codes like those found in Ephesians 5 for example. Rather than slapping a Christian bumper sticker of approval on the Greco-Roman household codes, Paul is actually *subverting* them (46–49). Evangelicals have misunderstood and ignored what Paul is trying to communicate. As another example, look at the amount of times Paul uses maternal language to describe himself (53). Such a view does not fit in standard evangelical frameworks. Barr then offers other typical accounts of passages like 1 Corinthians 14 that indicate the Pauline directives for silence are historically conditioned and not binding for today (63). Likewise, modern English translations have obscured women from the Bible by incorrect translations such as making Romans 16:7 mention Junius instead of Junia (67).

Chapter three is the most significant and unique contribution that Barr makes. It is about our "selective medieval memory." Barr retells the story of several medieval women, such as Margery Kempe, Saint Paula, Saint Margaret, and many others. Each of them "defied" male authority in various ways, such as responding directly to the archbishop that he needed to repent (73–74). Barr argues that these women "undermine" modern biblical womanhood. But they are "covered up, neglected, or retold to recast women as less significant than they really were" (84).

Chapter four considers the cost of the Reformation for women. While the Reformation is typically a story of triumph for Protestants, Barr suggests it was not so for women. The changes in the Reformation actually "hardened a theology of gender" that made their lives *tougher* (104). And it is because gender hierarchy has more to do with politics and economics than divine order that this is so obvious (106). Ultimately, the Reformation removed the priest and replaced him with the husband (117).

Chapter five then focuses on writing women out of the English Bible. Barr covers the gender inclusive debate with the NIV and how the ESV was a "direct response" to the debate (132). She shows that medieval Bibles were gender inclusive for accuracy and not cultural reasons (142). The reason the gender-inclusive medieval Bible's didn't persevere is because of culture. A move to using gender-inclusive language again, therefore, *restores* Scripture rather than distorts (148).

Chapter six examines how biblical womanhood "sanctifies subordination." Barr argues that after the Reformation the ideal of biblical womanhood and holiness changed from virginity to marriage (152). So, in a way, "the spiritual economy flipped" (153). Barr provides typical evangelical camp modesty examples to prove the oddness of evangelical views of holiness and purity for women. She also shows how the early modern period begins to link women's spiritual calling with the domestic life (159).

Chapter seven is Barr's attempt to argue that biblical womanhood has become gospel truth. She claims that the devil convinced evangelicals that biblical womanhood is central to the gospel (174). Evangelicals have forgotten the history of women in ministry and redefined holiness which has made biblical womanhood gospel truth (186). She provides two examples to prove how this has happened. First, she argues that the debate over inerrancy made biblical womanhood gospel truth. She says, "inerrancy introduced the ultimate justification for patriarchy" (190) and that "it became important because it provided a way to push women out of the pulpit" (191). Second, she argues that the growth of "Eternal Functional Subordination" (which she calls Arianism) is another example. Women's subordination is so important to evangelicals that they rewrote the Trinity to defend it (192).

Finally, chapter eight seeks to "set women free." Barr claims that "we can no longer deny a link between complementarianism and abuse." (207) Therefore, she pleads for a change to move forward. It is time to move on from complementarianism and the body count it has accrued.

3. What Barr Gets Right

I begin with what I find worthwhile in Barr's book because I want to lead with charity. While I find Barr's book deeply unsatisfying, I do think it has several points that deserve contemplation. First, I think her claim that the ideal of holiness has shifted for women in the modern era is both interesting and oftentimes true. She argues that holiness for modern women is now unduly linked *wholly* with domestic tasks. I think there is significant room for critique of how various sectors of evangelicalism have thought about gender roles, and reconsidering what holiness looks like for men and women is a worthy objective. I disagree with Barr's conclusions here but her claim that ideals of holiness can be culturally mutated is certainly true and worthy of contemplation.

Second, I think she raises criticisms of the "Piperesque" Council for Biblical Manhood and Womanhood (CBMW) crowd that are fair. For whatever reason, there are still conservative Evangelicals, even those in the Reformed adjacent sphere, who are advocating for the Eternal Functional Subordination (EFS) of the Son (I use "adjacent" purposefully—anyone who denies a basic tenant of what is held in common by the Reformed confessions *cannot,* by definition, be *Reformed*). While I have my problems with her historical retelling (as I will note briefly below), it's fair to criticize this doctrine and those who continue to either hold to it or pretend they never did hold to it. And we ought to examine *why* such a doctrine has held such a significant place for many. After all, I must confess, I too once believed in such a doctrine. But I was corrected through a course at—would you believe it?—*The* Southern Baptist Theological Seminary. It was there, in a course on the Person of Christ, during my MDiv, that I realized I was *wrong*. What I had grasped as fundamental for understanding male-female relations was actually a heterodox—possibly heretical—doctrine. But it is important to remember that many of these critiques of EFS have been rehashed *ad nauseum* over the last five years and roundly rejected by the majority of leading "complementarians." At this point, dogpiling on the minority EFS group can often be a cheap way to score points. But that doesn't negate its validity or prove that Barr is intending to do this. It is simply a note of caution for how we treat this topic as a "gotchya."

Third, I do think there is a needed conversation to be had around the abuses of authoritarian men (like Mark Driscoll and James MacDonald). I think work shining a light on these sorts of examples is important. And Barr does this to some extent in her work.

Fourth, I think her work in medieval history is both interesting and relevant. So much so that if her thesis was the modest claim that medieval church history should cause us to reexamine our cultural blind spots about how we think about gender, then I would probably *recommend* the book.

Fifth, I think she's a gifted writer. I don't mean this to sound pedantic or grasping at straws. She genuinely writes well and that deserves praise. From a purely stylistic perspective, I honestly enjoyed reading the book. Not many academics can write in such prose.

4. What Barr Gets Wrong

Now, charity does not require ignorance. Charity can critically interact. And whether you agree with the following critiques or not, I have labored to season them with grace and I hope you can sense that *ethos*. These debates too often devolve into tribal shouting. I hope to clear the air and level the playing field as best I can. There *are* ideas worth fighting for. There *are* ways to be sharpened by opposing interlocutors. We *can* be deadly serious and firm without being jerks. Now, I'm by no means the paradigmatic example for how to do this but I hope that I've run this through enough editorial checks to be closer to our Lord's instruction think with gentleness.

My first grievance is a typical one for philosophers. Barr's definitions of key terms throughout the book are either lacking, late, or convoluted. Take a crucial example in *complementarianism.* Barr considers complementarianism to be *identical* to patriarchy. She initially offers Judith Bennett's explanation of patriarchy that has three main meanings: 1) Male authority in the home, 2) Male ecclesiastical authority, and/or 3) Male authority in society. This seems like a fair way to cash out the various senses of patriarchy, but Barr, without reason, chooses to focus her study of complementarianism on the broadest and most expansive version of male authority as the target of her book: *universal* male authority in society (13-14). So, women are subordinate to men in *every* area. Elsewhere she confirms this definition by saying that complementarianism is "the theological view that women are divinely created as helpers and men are divinely created as leaders" (5). She says it means "women are called to secondary roles....in everything from sermons to Sunday school lessons" (1). The obvious problem with these definitions is that few complementarians would confess such a universal doctrine of male authority. Even those that pay lip service to such an idea would often say belief in a universal claim to male authority is a separate issue from male authority in the church and family. Male authority in society can be wrong and not implicate male authority in the church or family. So, from a purely definitional standpoint, she is bundling all sorts of diverse views that are separable from each other under one heading that ends up invalidating her thesis numerous times over. For an argument to be valid we need clear and precise definitions and categories. Lumping everyone into the same category is a recipe for a failed thesis. All I need is *one* counterexample to prove her thesis wrong with this definition. And I can provide numerous counterexamples—including myself!

But this is not all. Elsewhere she describes egalitarians as "those who argue for biblical equality between men and women" and complementarians as "those who argue for a biblical gender hierarchy that subordinates women to men" (32). But this is not a fair or clear definition. What does she mean by "biblical equality"? Is she begging the question here? It appears so. Because nearly all complementarians (if not all!) would vigorously claim that men and women have "biblical equality."

Consider one more example on the definitional front. She says that inerrancy is "the belief that the Bible is completely without error, including in areas of science and history" (188). But again, this definition is *unclear*. What does it mean for the Bible to be without error "including in areas of science and history"? Does she mean that what the Bible claims about science and history is *true*? That if the Bible speaks of a war in a certain year in a certain region that it *actually happened* in that year in that region? Or does she mean a more robust claim that historical and scientific claims outside of biblical revelation must be found somewhere in the Bible? That somehow the Bible contains every shred of historical and scientific piece of data? I assume she must mean the former. But it isn't clear and sets the reader up for possible confusion. If she means the latter, I worry that she isn't familiar with the strongest and *oldest* ways of understanding the role of Scripture in the Protestant tradition.

The second major problem with her book is expansive. I found legion of faulty "arguments" throughout. I even found logical fallacies ranging from strawmen to ad hominem to false causes to begging the question to appeals to emotion, among others. Now, it's true that as a philosopher I am more easily annoyed by invalid or unsound arguments. So, I may be more nitpicky than others (though, if I'm honest, I make the same mistakes too often myself). But that doesn't excuse them. Published work ought to be held to a higher standard. So, let me walk through twelve examples here, because I think this is both the reason the book is ultimately not recommendable *and* the greatest opportunity to learn to avoid certain mistakes. These are not in order of importance.

1. Barr says: "If men (simply because of their sex) have the potential to preach and exercise spiritual authority over a church congregation but women (simply because of their sex) do not, then that gives men 'in general' authority over women 'in general'" (18). Unfortunately, this argument isn't valid. There are premises smuggled into this argument that aren't listed. It is impossible to argue from particular situation X to general situation Y without further argument. Just because I think men because of their sex have the potential to preach and exercise authority over a church but women do not have the potential because of their sex does not entail that I think men have authority "in general" over women.

2. Barr makes an argument from the liberation of slaves to the liberation of women. Essentially, the argument is that if we can change our understanding there, why not here? (33–34). But for such an argument to work we would need significantly more explanation, examples, and proof. As it stands, it is unverifiable.

3. Barr questions "didn't the priesthood of all believers apply to women just as it applied to men?" (115). The point of her question is that if complementarians were consistent with their doctrine of the priesthood of all believers, then they would give up complementarianism. But of course, complementarianism has nothing to do with the priesthood of all believers doctrine. The doctrine of priesthood of all believers is about access to God and not formal pastoral offices. Therefore, a belief in one doctrine is not inconsistent with the other. If Barr wants to prove this argument, she needs to show the inconsistency clearly.

4. Barr explains that late medieval English sermons rarely preach the Pauline complementarian passages (e.g. 1 Tim 2; 1 Cor. 14). So, there isn't a continuous unbroken thread of teaching on women in the church like complementarians would like you to believe (44). There isn't some "golden chain" that you are somehow bucking against if you reject complementarianism. It is not part of the Great Tradition of the church. But the lack of medieval English sermons could be for numerous reasons—many of which would explain the lack rather than prove any point from silence. And Barr even later admits that "medieval preachers preached Paul, but their primary focus was to teach parishioners how to find

redemption through involvement in the sacraments and practices of the medieval Catholic Church" (119). Bingo. The reason they didn't emphasize these could be completely irrelevant to her argument.

5. Barr argues that Paul subverts the household codes. Therefore, complementarianism is wrong because complementarians think Paul didn't subvert the household codes (46–49). Well, yes. Yes, Paul does subvert the codes. Husbands have duties too. They ought to love their wives like Christ loves the church. A radical calling. But does anyone disagree? Has Barr taken the time to read anyone besides Piper, Grudem, Ware, and Dobson to confirm this? Or have Owen Strachan's blogs and Denny Burk's tweets (yes, tweets) been sufficient evidence? Moreover, I don't think any of them would disagree here. Complementarians do not find the household codes to be simply God anointing the ancient context with complete inerrancy. Take nearly any serious complementarian commentary off the shelf and read the section from Ephesians 5 and you will see an overwhelming consensus here.

6. Barr argues that the English translators of the Bible have intentionally obscured women leadership. For example, take Romans 16:1: "I commend to you our sister Phoebe, a servant of the church at Cenchreae" (ESV). If the word for "servant" here were attached to a masculine name instead of feminine, translators would make Phoebe out to be a deacon instead of a servant (65–66). But that's not true. Look even at her favorite whipping boy, the ESV. In Colossians 4:12 Epaphras is a servant even when it's the same word Phoebe was described as (transliterated as deacon). Of course, Paul and James are "servants" throughout their letters too. The word "deacon" is used in the ESV in only two places: 1 Timothy 3 and Philippians 1:1 when paired with the office of elder. Nowhere else is it used. Not of men. Not of women. So, Barr's entire argument here rests on either a misunderstanding or ignorance.

7. Barr argues that Junia is an apostle in Romans 16:7 (66–67). If she is an apostle, complementarianism is wrong. But few take Andronicus to be an apostle (the guy listed next to her in Romans). The phrase that is crucial is …οἵτινές εἰσιν ἐπίσημοι ἐν τοῖς ἀποστόλοις… The operative preposition that needs clarity is ἐν. The text reads "Who is well known ἐν the apostles." Clearly, the interpretation hinges on how we translate ἐν. The name of the person being masculine (Junius) or feminine (Junia) is irrelevant. And if you know Greek, you know ἐν is incredibly elastic. There is no obvious meaning. You need the context. So, it's going to be an interpretive decision no matter how you look at it. Either, as an egalitarian, you'll take your presuppositions and cram them into the ἐν or, as

a complementarian, you'll do the same. This isn't meant to be bad. None of us can theologize or even translate in a vacuum. But it is important to note that this isn't some obvious translation decision. Anyone telling you otherwise likely has an agenda to maintain.

8. Repeatedly Barr gives examples of women deacons as proof that complementarianism is wrong. For example, she makes a big point out of Chrysostom saying women can be deacons (67-68). But this isn't unique to Chrysostom. The Associate Reformed Presbyterians (ARP) is complementarian and allows for women deacons. As do "complementarian" macho groups like Acts29. But Barr says women deacons are a "frank understanding of female leadership." (68). However, a strong understanding of the office of deacon would recognize it is not an office of leadership. Deacons are about service. Finding female deacons invalidates nothing of the complementarian perspective. Which is precisely why you see them in complementarian churches.

9. Barr argues that Mary Magdalene is preaching after the resurrection which is proof complementarianism is wrong (87). Other women, like Hildegard of Bingen took "preaching tours" which proves complementarianism is wrong (no preaching for women, they say) (89). But this simply isn't preaching. Sharing the good news in informal settings isn't preaching. To prove that it was preaching would require an extended excursus and definition. But nowhere do we find one. All that is found is an assumption that we all agree about what preaching is. But the Reformed tradition has a very specific understanding of the task of preaching that is linked to the office of elder (and gifted brothers for the 2LCF) and the Lord's Day. In a similar argument, Barr shows that Genovefa (a female) established Paris as a Christian stronghold "just as effectively as male bishops" (89). Therefore, women were doing the same stuff as men. Ergo, complementarianism in the modern sense is false. But rather than proof of a faulty belief in complementarianism, these are repeated evidences of a lack of understanding of church polity and the church offices. It is pragmatism devoid of polity. If Barr wanted to convince Reformed theologians at least, she would need to work within their theological framework, which she does not. And maybe she would object at this point and say "That's exactly right. I'm not arguing against them." But I would reply: "Okay, that's fine. You don't have to. But you need to if you want your thesis to stick. Knocking down the weakest arguments won't win your case."

10. Barr claims that "as a church historian, I immediately recognized the eternal subordination of the Son as Arianism" and that the entire Christian world reacted with "horror" to Arianism (194). The reason she brings this up as a knock against complementarianism is because CBMW has been a major

proponent of EFS. But there are two major problems here. First, CBMW is not the only representative of complementarianism. In fact, they aren't even the majority. They are a modern invention and a minority segment. Knocking them out doesn't knock out complementarianism. EFS is a new invention that has never been linked to complementarianism in the past nor need it be in the future. Second, EFS isn't Arianism. While Barr is no doubt confident in her assertion, it's simply not true. Arianism argues that the Son is a different substance than the Father and is created, but EFS decidedly does not. And of course, her anecdote, as noted by DeYoung, that the whole Christian world was "horrified" by Arius and his views is alarming because it's so ignorant of the historical outworking of the debate. In actuality, much of the world was the opposite of horrified.

11. Barr holds up Saint Paula as an exemplar. Barr retells Paula's story about how she abandoned her children for the "higher purpose of following God's call on her life". After the death of her husband, she left her children "alone, crying on the shore" setting out to serve God (79). By my lights, this is not a story to be emulated, admired, or promoted. This is a story of direct disobedience to God's will for parents to care for, love, and provide for their children. Paul tells us that a failure to provide for one's family is worse than being an unbeliever (1 Tim. 5:8). To think that this is even remotely near a positive example is extremely concerning. To be frank: I don't care if she helped translate a Bible. The ends never justify the means. We are not utilitarians.

12. Finally, Barr notes that "Patriarchy walks with structural racism and systemic oppression, and it has done so consistently throughout history" (33). I note this because it smacks of the faddishness with which some arguments can be made. I say this because modern race studies suggest that racism is to be a social construct born alongside America. If that is true, patriarchy is only a few centuries old. My point here is that Barr seems to be hitching her thesis to a popular "obvious" cause to give further weight to it. But what would have given it more weight? Examples outside America and England. Where is Africa, Russia, Vietnam, and China within her book? Where are the patristic sources? They aren't there. And it's true that she is a medieval expert. So of course, she doesn't miss the medievals. But her thesis is universal. If it's going to be universal like this, it needs to reckon with universal experience and belief and not argue from the particular to the universal.

The third major issue I had with the book is that her historical retelling is often suspect. I don't want to rehash what DeYoung discussed in his review. So, I'll keep this short and point to an example he didn't mention. Consider Hanserd Knollys. She describes Katherine Sutton and how she began to "preach and prophesy through singing" and that Pastor Knollys supported her. Therefore, she says that women had the *right* to preach and prophesy according to Knollys (182–183). But this ignores the historical context about the serious debate over singing in the Particular Baptist churches at this time. It also ignores the argument from Knollys that there was a distinct "ordinance" of praise and signing. Sutton possessed this anointing for *singing.*[1] Singing was *decidedly* different from pastoral *preaching.* This is either deceitful or sloppy historical work from Barr. I hesitate to imply deceit on anyone's behalf, but Barr is a well-trained historian, so I have a difficult time understanding why this claim was made.

As a final point of issue, I must confess, I think the tribal wars are only incited within this book. Instead of attempting to *persuade* those who disagree, Barr often pours gasoline and lights a match. Now, I bet if I asked Barr in person if she meant what she wrote in what I'm going to quote, she would likely retract it or modify it in some way (and I did email this to her beforehand in hopes to understand, but received no reply). But consider a few examples without my commentary first (though I will bold certain key words and phrases for emphasis):

- "So much textual and historical evidence counters the complementarian model of biblical womanhood and the theology behind it. Sometimes I am **dumbfounded** that this is a battle we are still fighting." (6)

- "Ironically, complementarian theology claims it is defending a plan and natural interpretation of the Bible while really it is defending an interpretation that has been corrupted by our sinful human drive to **dominate** others and build hierarchies of power and **oppression. I can't think of anything less Christlike than hierarchies like these.**" (7)

- "The truth—the evangelical reality—is that we have focused so much on adapting Paul to be like us that we have forgotten to adapt ourselves to what Paul is calling us to be: one in Christ. Instead of choosing the better part and embracing the "new world of the Christ-crucified gospel," we have chosen to keep doing what humans have always done: **building our own tower of power and hierarchy.**" (42)

---

1 Matthew Ward, *Pure Worship: The Early English Baptist Distinctive* (Eugene, OR: Pickwick Publications, 2014), 175.

- [Why are evangelicals complementarian?] "to protect and enhance the **authority** of men." (99)

- "the greatest trick **the devil** ever pulled was convincing Christians that **oppression is godly**....That women's subordination is central to the gospel of Christ." (173)

- "When evangelicals have supported women in public ministry, they are most closely aligned with the gospel of Jesus. It is when evangelicals **succumb to the peer pressure** of contemporary culture that they turn against women in public ministry." (179)

- [Complementarians are in a] "**blind pursuit** to maintain **control** over women" (194)

It is astounding that such rhetoric is used against theological "opponents." Note first that these sorts of claims are a substitute for an argument. They attempt to win an argument by force of emotion. These claims are never *proven.* They are asserted. Note second that these claims assume a significant number of beliefs on the part of "complementarians." They are in a "blind pursuit" to control women. It nearly sounds as if complementarians are wild and ravenous *animals.* They are deceived by the devil himself. The only reason they are complementarians is to oppress women. There is *nothing* less Christlike than to be a complementarian. But I think most fair readers will recognize this isn't true (and as I suggested, I've got to imagine *she* doesn't think this is true, either). Would she say both her and her husband were in blind pursuits to oppress women and were deceived by the devil prior to rejecting complementarianism? Or would Barr be willing to ask my own wife if I was in a blood thirsty lust to dominate her? I doubt it. The rhetoric here is not only unfair but inflammatory and slanderous. It ought to be retracted and apologized for. Now, true, there are instances where this may be the case. But she doesn't limit her claims. They are *universal* and they are peppered throughout her book. They are not rare. And if you believe charity is a virtue, we ought to take people at their word. Consider my own plea: why am I a complementarian? Because I believe I am bound by Scripture to be one. Not because of culture. Not because of ambition. Not because of a desire to dominate and oppress. Not because of *anything.* I simply want to be faithful to the Bible and I have no other way of seeing texts such as 1 Timothy 2 without violating my conscience.

5. Conclusion

I think it's fairly obvious by this point what my opinion of Barr's book is. It isn't great. It's not good, either, unfortunately. I honestly *wanted* it to be good. I *wanted* to learn about the historical shifts that have come about with modern evangelicalism and complementarianism. I *wanted* to learn about the history of the church and its thoughts and practices on the topic. I really, truly, and honestly *wanted* this book to be good. But while I did learn about some obscure medieval women, I didn't learn much of anything else. And it's a real shame. There *is* a great need for a book on this topic. But this is not the one. So, again, I simply cannot recommend the book as worthwhile reading. I hate being the big bad mean reviewer here, but I am bound to confess the truth. And Barr's book simply doesn't provide a faithful interaction with "biblical womanhood" or a serious critique of it. I think there is needed space for such a book in the future, but hopefully it won't make these same mistakes.

Book Review:
The Failure of Natural Theology

Johnson, Jeffrey D. *The Failure of Natural Theology: A Critical Appraisal of the Philosophical Theology of Thomas Aquinas*. Conway, AR: Free Grace Press Academic, 2021. 264pp. Softcover. ISBN: 9781952599378. $40.00.

Reviewed by Jordan L. Steffaniak, ThM

1. Introducing Johnson and His Project

Jeffrey D. Johnson's latest release from his publishing arm is *The Failure of Natural Theology*. The book, as the title suggests, is controversial. While there has been a steady rise in appreciation for Thomistic theology, especially on the doctrine of God, Johnson seeks to end this growing movement. If you aren't familiar with Johnson, he is the Pastor of preaching and teaching at Grace Bible Church and President of Grace Bible Theological Seminary in Conway, Arkansas. He has an M. Rel. in Biblical Studies from Central Baptist College and a D. Min. from Veritas Theological Seminary.[1] Johnson has published widely through his publishing house, Free Grace Press, on a variety of topics.

Before summarizing and interacting with Johnson's work, I should answer two questions. **First,** what is my evaluation of his book (in other words, what is the "TL;DR" version)? I must confess that Johnson's book is, to borrow his own phrase, *fatally flawed*. It's flawed in its claims, its argumentation, and its rigor. If I were to critically engage all the flaws, this review would become a book of its own. So, I would warn you not to purchase and read the book. It does not contribute to the ongoing debate about the validity and value of Thomism. Its greatest flaw is a misunderstanding of natural theology. But it also fails to make a serious and convincing case for Neo-Classical Theism. However, my intent is not mere macho tribal posturing that results in little more than beating one's chest for their

---

[1] I should note that I am not sure if Johnson holds a Th. D. or a D. Min. His church website indicates he holds a Th.D. but his seminary website indicates that he holds a D. Min. His degree granting institution does not offer a Th. D. Thus, I have assumed his actual degree is a D. Min.

team, which leads to my **second** question: why have I chosen to critically review this book given my belief that it is neither serious scholarship nor persuasive in its claims? Johnson is not an expert in natural theology, Thomism, Philosophy of Religion, or the Doctrine of God. He has not published in this area in any peer-reviewed work. So, why give it attention? While I do think there is always a worry that if you review books that you find seriously problematic, you will inadvertently make them *more* popular and *more* widely read than they deserve, I think this book warrants attention for two reasons.

The first reason I find it important to review is that it's written by a self-attesting confessor of the Second London Confession of Faith (2LCF) that is the President of a seminary that is growing in popularity among those that outwardly seek to confess 2LCF. I find this very troubling. The reason being, as I will argue, Johnson denies 2LCF at crucial points in his book (This isn't a worry for those not committed to confessing 2LCF or Classical Theism, so if that's you, feel free to ignore this point). Moreover, I am a firm believer that we should be more critical of our own "tribe" and Johnson fits that label for me since I confess 2LCF. I think we should reserve our strongest critiques for those that outwardly confess the same beliefs. As Proverbs remind us, "faithful are the wounds of a friend." This doesn't mean my goal is to *wound* in the contemporary sense. I seek to build up faith, hope, and love in both Johnson and his readers. But these virtues compel me to provide a critical engagement in hope that bad arguments would be surrendered, false beliefs would be revised, and faith in our God would be nourished.

The second reason I find it worthwhile to review the book (and more relevant for those who find the rise in Thomistic allegiance troubling) is that critically engaging with primary and secondary sources and showing how to properly evaluate evidence and arguments is of great value and short supply. Many of us learn best from serious disagreement and debate. The kind of debate that focuses on arguments and asks the hard questions. And Johnson *does* ask some good questions. It's hard to say it better than Richard Cross, who reminds us that "we learn from the mistakes of our forebears as much as from their successes."[2] I hope to provide this sort of educational interaction within my critical engagement. This ought to remind us that people and books are *not* enemies to be conquered but (potential) friends to be persuaded. As I note later in my

---

2   Richard Cross, *The Metaphysics of the Incarnation: Thomas Aquinas to Duns Scotus* (Oxford: Oxford University Press, 2005), vii-viii.

review, I find Johnson to be both earnest and genuine in his thinking. But I find his arguments seriously wanting. To his work I now turn.

2. Summarizing the "Failure" of Natural Theology

If the subtitle of the book wasn't clear enough, Johnson sets out to critique Thomas Aquinas and his natural theology. In Johnson's introduction, he explains that Thomas's doctrine of God is wrong and "problematic for a proper view of classical theism" (4). He then provides his basic thesis:

> When Thomas Aquinas introduced Aristotelian concepts into his theology proper, however, he not only departed from the theologians who went before him but he also altered the biblical teaching of God. As this book will seek to demonstrate, Thomas added to God's simple and immutable nature an additional attribute not taught in the Scriptures: divine immobility (5).

In short, Johnson suggests that by integrating philosophical categories outside of Scripture, Thomas, and those like him, err.

Johnson structures his argument around this thesis, covering nine total chapters with two appendices. Each chapter begins with several biographical paragraphs about Thomas that are supposed to orient the reader to the topic of the chapter. The first two chapters focus on problems with "natural theology" and "philosophy." Johnson argues that natural theology is a human project designed to understand God apart from divine revelation (10–11). He suggests that natural theology is distinct from natural revelation which starts and ends with God's self-disclosure (11). He spans several pages attempting to show this distinction. Based on this, he waxes about the inability of natural theology to reconcile the transcendence and immanence of God. The following two chapters are dedicated to elucidating the natural theology of Aristotle and Pseudo-Dionysius. Johnson spends a significant amount of time summarizing Aristotle's account of motion and his cosmological argument. He then focuses primarily on the mysticism of Pseudo-Dionysius.

From this foundation he then has two chapters examining Thomas Aquinas's philosophical theology. He summarizes the various epistemological methods for knowing God, the role of philosophy, divine immobility, and more. He then suggests that *contra* Thomas and Aristotle, "both non-motion and motion" can exist in God *as Trinity* (116). Afterward, his seventh chapter, focuses on the main problem within his thesis: a critique of "divine immobility." He claims that Thomas *added* the attribute of "divine immobility" to God because of his commitment to Aristotelean metaphysics (136). The next chapter attempts to provide the "solution" to the problem: the Trinity. Herein, Johnson argues that "simplicity is not ultimate," suggesting that Thomas forced all theological data to fit a strong version of divine simplicity at the expense of the Trinity (154). Finally, he closes with a chapter on analogical language. He worries that the Thomistic version of analogy forces God to be wholly other, on the other side of a "transcendental wall" that is impossible to cross (177).

3. Three Serious Criticisms

Admittedly, this is a short summary. Much more could be said. But I think it gets the basic idea across and I think my critical interaction will further elucidate Johnson's argument. There are three main areas I plan to critique, though there are numerous aspects I take issue with. The overarching problem that I think infects each is *misunderstanding*. I think Johnson misunderstands natural theology, he misunderstands Thomas *and* classical theism, and he misunderstands his own interlocutors will survey each of these areas in turn. As a note, it is important to point out that I think Johnson's own flaw *isn't malicious*. I genuinely believe he is seeking to be faithful to Christ, his church, and his Word. I believe he is doing his best to read Thomas and understand him. *However,* this does not absolve one from guilt, especially when that one publishes an entire book length work based on misunderstanding. In the end, I found myself sympathizing with Johnson's claim that "it is frustrating reading Aquinas because he leads his readers into a maze of irresolvable contradictions" (150). I sympathize because I found myself frustrated reading *Johnson* for the same reasons.

3.1 The Problem of Natural Theology

The first problem I focus on is this: Johnson's "fatal flaw" of natural theology isn't fatal. The reason it's not fatal is because he misunderstands natural theology. He defines natural theology narrowly as a project that is completely divorced and insulated from divine revelation. For example, he says "natural theology is the philosophy of religion, and the philosophy of religion is limited to what can be known about God through reason or empirical senses" (11). He thinks natural theology *must* start somewhere *other than* God's self-disclosure. He claims it "seeks to construct a knowledge of God through reason and sense experience" alone (11). He thinks "natural theology seeks to obtain a philosophical knowledge of God by suppressing the knowledge of God that comes through natural revelation" (22). But these claims are false. Not only are they false, some are potentially slanderous. Does he *really* think that those committed to retrieving Thomism (and all other philosophical theology) are actively *"suppressing"* that knowledge of God? It is one thing to say they suppress it passively by entailment (wrong as it may be). But to suggest they are *actively* doing so is serious defamation.

Now, it *is* true, that there is a branch of natural theology that is preoccupied with various arguments for the existence of God apart from Scripture in many cases, which is the scope of natural theology I think Johnson is usually targeting (though it's not always clear). But even these arguments are constructed within the context of faith seeking understanding and never divorced from God's revelation. Take Anselm as a chief example. He admittedly seeks to construct an argument apart from divine revelation, but *not* in contradiction to it nor in ignorance of it. There is a massive difference between conceiving of something apart from Y and in contradiction to Y. One does not entail the other. More importantly, natural theology as an entire project is not identical to these sorts of ventures. I have written elsewhere about the nature of natural theology, and I follow Herman Bavinck that defines it as theology that is "through" the natural order compared to supernatural theology (like Scripture) that is "from beyond" the natural order.[3] The task of natural theology is to utilize natural means via our renewed reason in service of theological construction under the authority of Scripture and guidance of the Holy Spirit. Natural theology is not some hyper-speculative enterprise designed to insulate oneself from God's divine revelation in Scripture. Thus, I think Johnson fundamentally misunderstands the theological task which leads him to his faulty conclusion.

I think much of the underlying reason for Johnson's failure to understand this is due to a naïve biblicism. For example, Johnson critiques Thomas because his "doctrine of God is not rooted in revelation alone." He claims this ends up being an "an inadvertent attack on the sufficiency of divine revelation" (48). This misunderstanding of Scripture's sufficiency is a problem that is surfacing in more than discussions on the doctrine of God, so it is good to think about what sufficiency means. 2LCF 1.1 confesses the following: "The Holy Scripture is the only sufficient, certain, and infallible

---

3   Jordan L. Steffaniak, "The God of All Creation: A Critique of Evangelical Biblicism and Recovery of Perfect Being Theology," *Journal of Reformed Theology* 14, no. 4 (December 1, 2020): 360, https://doi.org/10.1163/15697312-bja10008; Herman Bavinck, *Reformed Dogmatics*, ed. John Bolt, trans. John Vriend (Grand Rapids: Baker Academic, 2003), 1:307.

rule of all **saving knowledge, faith,** and **obedience...**" Notice what is sufficient. Is it *everything*? No. It is not sufficient for changing the oil on my truck. It is not sufficient for installing a new hard drive in my computer. It is sufficient for saving knowledge, faith, and obedience. Everything necessary for the Christian life is found in the Bible. But not every detail of the faith is there. And utilizing philosophy (such as "good and necessary consequence") does not jeopardize Scripture's sufficiency. It does not move the foundation from divine revelation to human reasoning. The theological task is not to merely parrot the words of Scripture but to "think God's thoughts after him and to trace their unity" as Bavinck has said.[4] The church catholic has understood this—including the vast number of Reformed theologians— and even Thomas himself. For example, Thomas argues that "This science [theology] can take something from the philosophical disciplines not because it necessarily needs their help, but rather in order to achieve greater clarity regarding its own proper subject matter."[5] Elsewhere, again, Thomas says, "whatever is found in other sciences that is inconsistent with the truth of this science is to be condemned as utterly false"[6] Neither Thomas, nor the Reformed, thought philosophy was superior to Scripture. But both found it *necessary* to come to a clearer understanding of it.

But there is a further problem with Johnson's understanding of natural theology. At times, he seems to think *philosophy* is interchangeable with natural theology. He even argues that "Philosophy, as it turns out, is a detractor rather than a handmaiden to theology" (191). To be frank, I'm not sure what to do with this claim. His entire book is an exercise in *philosophical* theology. Making arguments is part of what *philosophy* is. So, either Johnson's claim is entirely self-defeating or he is incredibly unclear and means to say that something like *Aristotelian* or *Thomistic* philosophy is a detractor.

3.2 The Problem of Thomism and Classical Theism

The second major error that Johnson commits is a fundamental misunderstanding of both Thomas and Classical Theism. Both errors are intertwined to some extent, but I will try to show his mistakes related to each separately.

---

4   Bavinck, *RD*, 1:44.
5   Thomas Aquinas, *The Treatise on the Divine Nature: Summa Theologiae* I, 1–13, trans. Brian J. Shanley, The Hackett Aquinas (Indianapolis: Hackett, 2006), I 1.5 ad 2.
6   Aquinas, *Treatise on the Divine Nature*, I 1.6 ad 2.

3.2.1 Thomas Vindicated

I intend to focus first on one of Johnson's most egregious errors when handling Thomas since I have already interacted with his misunderstanding of natural theology. The error I want to expose here is related to Johnson's "fatal flaw" for Thomas—what he calls the additional attribute of "divine immobility." It is this "divine attribute" that Johnson suggests Thomas *adds* to the divine nature and signals his unorthodoxy (5). Johnson builds his case against divine immobility by summarizing Aristotle's cosmological argument for an unmoved mover. Here is how he sets it up in his own words:

> According to Aristotle, since all things in motion have an external cause, there must be something without motion that is the first cause, and this static, stationary, and immobile first cause Aristotle defined as actus purus (55).

So, since Thomas sought to "baptize Aristotle," he follows Aristotle in this argument, which means that God as first cause must be "static, stationary, and immobile." Even in God's action to create he "remains completely passive and unaware that he is exciting objects to move after him" (64). So, Johnson's basic argument against Thomas is as follows: "If everything in motion has a cause, and if God is first cause, then God must be immobile" (97). Let me spell that out a little clearer:

1. Everything in motion has a cause

2. If everything has a cause, there would be an infinite regress of causes

3. Therefore, there must be a first cause that isn't in motion (from 1 and 2)

4. God is the first cause

5. An object that isn't in motion is immobile (i.e. static and stationary)

6. Therefore, God isn't in motion and is immobile (from 4 and 5)

There are a few curious things about this argument. First, Johnson's own solution to this argument is to deny 1 and 3. His reason for denying 1 appears to be that physics doesn't map onto metaphysics. What is true for this cosmos is not true for the divine. So, not every motion has a cause (133). His reason for denying 3 is a little stranger. He says: "Who is to say both non-motion and motion couldn't exist in the Trinity?" (116). Who is to say? Well, classical logic is to say that A can't be non-A and be true. That's like saying 2+2=5. Maybe Johnson would want to make use of sub-classical logic, but I doubt he is aware of the ongoings of such a niche and complicated subject. But maybe this was a slip of the tongue and what he really meant to say was that in God there is *self-motion*. Thus, God isn't caused from anything external to move but is moved by his own good pleasure. But even if this is Johnson's argument, it doesn't invalidate the Thomistic proof. Johnson is not attentive to the debates regarding what Thomas means in the first way (e.g. the cosmological argument for an unmoved mover). There is debate over whether motion is intransitive or passive. For example, does Thomas mean that **anything** that is in motion is moved by another *or* that anything that is **passively** moved by something else is moved by another? There is a strong Thomistic consensus that the passive sense is the proper meaning, which then excludes self-motion from the proof.[7] In which case, Johnson's argument is invalid from the start.

However, these aren't the only problems. Johnson's understanding of what immobility means is wrong. He thinks immobility means being static or stationary. He claims that an unmoved mover couldn't *do* anything—it would be frozen (66).[8] But this is the exact critique Karl Barth suggested over a half century ago: "The pure *immobile* is death. If, then, the pure *immobile* is God, death is God."[9] It reminds me of Charles Hartshorne as well who is preoccupied with the nastiness of "immobility." But it should be obvious that Thomas *doesn't* argue that God is immobile in the sense of being passive, unaware, and static. Rather, it's part of what *actus purus* means for God to be the most active being with the *most* life. Therefore, God is not immobile in the sense of a lifeless rock but immobile in the sense of possessing so much life in pure perfection that he cannot possibly be moved to receive further life. Thomas sums up his understanding of motion and mobility in fairly clear terms:

> Augustine is speaking here according to the manner in which Plato said that the first mover moves itself, referring to every activity as a motion; on this usage, even to know, to will, and to love are described as some kind of motion. Hence because God knows and loves himself, they accordingly said that God moves himself; but this is not the motion or change of what exists in potentiality, which is the sort of motion we are talking about in this discussion."[10]

---

7   Timothy Pawl, "The Five Ways," in *The Oxford Handbook of Aquinas,* ed. Brian Davies and Eleonore Stump (Oxford: Oxford University Press, 2014), 116.

8   It is worth noting that Johnson does admits that the Thomistic vision of God doesn't mean he isn't *doing* anything. Johnson says, "it just means that whatever God does, he is doing in an undifferentiated, single, necessary, timeless, and ever-present act" (119).

9   Karl Barth, *Church Dogmatics,* trans. T. H. L. Parker, vol. II/1 (Edinburgh: T & T Clark, 1957), 494.

10   Aquinas, *The Treatise on the Divine Nature,* I 9.1 ad 1.

James Dolezal echoes Thomas: "God is unmoved not because he lacks life and action, but because he is identical with his life and actuality and therefore cannot be determined to any further actuality of life than he already has."[11] To claim that immobility is identical to inactivity is a fundamental misunderstanding and devastating to Johnson's case.

But Johnson's reasoning for immobility defined as static has one more faulty argument. He thinks that God as *actus purus* would mean that God cannot create because creation is an efficient cause and efficient causation requires movement (68). But, again, this shows a lack of careful attention to Thomas. Thomas explicitly calls God the first efficient cause.[12] And for Thomas, an efficient cause is "that which brings something into being or changes it in some way."[13] There is no reason that God as efficient cause should require motion. To assume motion is required for efficient causation is to beg the question against Thomas. While Thomas could be wrong, it's necessary to at least give him a fair hearing. For example, Thomas explains this very scenario in consecutive sections of his *Summa Contra Gentiles:*

> All motion or change is the act of that which exists potentially, as such. But in the action which is creation, nothing potential pre-exists to receive the action, as we have just shown. Therefore, creation is not a motion or a change.... Again, in every change or motion there must be something existing in one way now and in a different way before, for the very word change shows this.14

> For creation is not a change, but the very dependency of the created act of being upon the principle from which it is produced. And thus, creation is a kind of relation; so that nothing prevents its being in the creature as its subject.[15]

Both of these sections clearly offer a model of understanding how God can be pure act and can create without motion.

3.2.2 Classical Theism Vindicated

Johnson not only misunderstands Thomas but Classical Theism itself. There are four areas I want to focus on here. I count these as misunderstandings and

---

11   James E. Dolezal, *God Without Parts: Divine Simplicity and the Metaphysics of God's Absoluteness* (Eugene, OR: Pickwick, 2011), 86–87.
12   Aquinas, *The Treatise on the Divine Nature,* I 3.8c.
13   Edward Feser, *Scholastic Metaphysics: A Contemporary Introduction,* Editiones Scholasticae 39 (Heusenstamm: Ed. Scholasticae, 2014), 42.
14   Thomas Aquinas, *Summa Contra Gentiles: Book Two: Creation,* trans. James F. Anderson (Notre Dame, IN: Notre Dame University Press, 1975), 17.
15   Aquinas, *Summa Contra Gentiles,* 18.

not just bad arguments because he claims to confess 2LCF which confesses Classical Theism and because there are *good* arguments out there against Classical Theism. I don't take those arguments to be persuasive, but they are compelling in their own ways.

First, Johnson rejects the traditional account of divine simplicity because he rejects that God's attributes are identical with one another. For example, Johnson rejects that God's knowledge is identical to his essence and rejects that God's knowledge and will are identical (131, 140). He thinks that "if God can distinguish between particular things outside of himself, then he is no longer undifferentiated in his simplicity" (132). He says that God has "ontological complexity" (50). Furthermore, he thinks that the Thomistic account of simplicity requires creation to be necessary and eternal (119, 125). His arguments main contention is a rudimentary version of R. T. Mullins, *Simply Impossible: A Case Against Divine Simplicity*. Now, I think Johnson does press on an important possible problem for the Thomistic account. However, his "solution" not only ignores the tradition's answers but departs from the tradition itself. For example, Thomas addresses the problem of necessity. He seeks to circumvent the problem by positing two senses of necessity—one that is hypothetical and one that is absolute. It is only the hypothetical necessity that applies to creation and such a sense of necessity does not lead to an absolutely necessary or eternal creation.16 But Johnson does not engage such possible rebuttals.

A second area of misunderstanding is the doctrine of immutability. Consider Johnson's criticism of Thomas: "Aquinas taught that God is not just immutable in his character but also in his actions (i.e., immobile)" (120). This claim reveals that Johnson thinks of immutability as a changelessness of *character* and *not* action. Such a view is defensible, but it isn't Classical Theism or 2LCF. For example, it is ubiquitous in the Reformed tradition to speak of God as being immutable in more than mere essence or character. Consider just a few examples. 2LCF 2.1 confesses that God is both immutable in essence and *will* and 2LCF 3.5 speaks of God's immutable purpose. Francis Turretin explains that "immutability is an incommunicable attribute of God by which is denied of him not only all change, but also all possibility of change, as much with respect to existence as to will."17 Petrus van Mastricht similarly

---

16 See Tyler Wittman, *God and Creation in the Theology of Thomas Aquinas and Karl Barth* (New York: Cambridge University Press, 2019), 84–91.

17 Francis Turretin, *Institutes of Elenctic Theology*, ed. James T. Dennison, trans. George Musgrave Giger (Phillipsburg, NJ: P&R, 1994), 1:204.

says that God is "entirely and in all ways immutable."[18] Herman Bavinck follows them, claiming that "God is as immutable in his knowing, willing, and decreeing as he is in his being."[19] Even Louis Berkhof agrees, saying that "The immutability of God is a necessary concomitant of His aseity. It is that perfection of God by which He is devoid of all change, not only in His Being, but also in His perfections, and in His purposes and promises."[20]

A third area of misunderstanding is that Johnson sounds like a Social Trinitarian at times. Johnson says that there is "internal *(ad intra)* movement within the Godhead" (116). He also says that each of the Triune persons "have their own distinct self-awareness" (185). That's just Social Trinitarianism. If Johnson doesn't mean to affirm this, he is being sloppy with his language. Now, again, you who are reading this review might be a Social Trinitarian. That's fine! I'm not here to argue about that. But I *do* think it's fairly obvious that Social Trinitarianism is irreconcilable with 2LCF and Classical Theism.

A fourth area of misunderstanding is the nature of "divine relations." Johnson asks, "How can God know and love that with which he has no real relation?" (133). Johnson is referring to the classic Thomistic doctrine that God has no "real relation" with creation. But Johnson evidences a lack of understanding regarding what this "real" is supposed to mean. It *doesn't* mean having an especially intimate relation with something. It has a technical meaning. There are two conditions that are required for something to be a "real relation" for Thomas:

1. The relation must be between two really distinct extra-mental things
2. The relation must have a real extra-mental foundation *in* the subjects.[21]

So, the reason God doesn't have a *real* relation with creation isn't about intimacy or love or anything else. It's a metaphysical claim. It only means that there isn't a real extra-mental foundation *in* God for his relation to creation. He is *really* related to it in the sense that he loves and cares and provides in *reality*. But he isn't related to it in a way that creation changes him intrinsically.

A fifth area of misunderstanding is concerning traditional language about God. Johnson thinks that if we understand language about God as "restricted to the use of earthly symbols and physical metaphors" that we lock the real God behind a "transcendental wall." He thinks such an

---

18 Petrus van Mastricht, *Theoretical-Practical Theology*, ed. Joel R. Beeke, trans. Todd M. Rester (Grand Rapids: Reformation Heritage Books, 2018), 2:155.
19 Bavinck, *RD*, 1:154.
20 Louis Berkhof, *Systematic Theology* (Louisville: GLH, 2017), 37.
21 Mark Gerald Henninger, *Relations: Medieval Theories,* 1250–1325 (New York: Oxford University Press, 1989), 7.

approach makes love, mercy, and compassion "merely anthropomorphic" (148). But this is just how the entire classical tradition has thought about language for God. Take two examples, though I could provide legion. First, John Chrysostom thinks that because God is ineffable he is "beyond our intelligence, invisible, incomprehensible" and "transcends the power of mortal words."[22] Chrysostom takes this to mean that the only way for humans to understand God is if he condescends and *accommodates* himself. As Chrysostom explains:

> God condescends whenever he is not seen as he is, but in the way one incapable of beholding him is able to look upon him. In this way God reveals himself by accommodating what he reveals to the weakness of vision of those who behold him.[23]

Chrysostom is saying that our language about God is bound to the created realm and ultimately lacks transcendent correspondence. Second, John Calvin emphasizes the nature of accommodated language so much that it might be *the* chief facet of his theology of revelation.[24] Calvin follows the logic of Chrysostom and claims that God reveals knowledge "tempered to our feeble comprehension."[25] He explains in full:

> For because our weakness does not attain to his exalted state, the description of him that is given to us must be accommodated to our capacity so that we may understand. Now the mode of accommodation is for him to represent himself to us not as he is in himself, but as he seems to us.[26]

So, for both Calvin and Chrysostom, our knowledge of God is accommodated knowledge. It is *necessarily* limited to the created realm. But our language being creaturely and imperfect doesn't mean that we are trapped behind a transcendental wall.

Now, I want to summarize the overarching problem I am addressing in this section. It is *not* about the validity of Classical Theism *per se*. Rather, it

---

22 John Chrysostom, *On the Incomprehensible Nature of God*, trans. Paul W. Harkins (Washington D.C.: Catholic University of America Press, 1984), III, 5.

23 Chrysostom, *On the Incomprehensible Nature of God*, III, 15.

24 Michael Horton, "Knowing God: Calvin's Understanding of Revelation," in *John Calvin and Evangelical Theology: Legacy and Prospect*, ed. Sung Wook Chung (Louisville: Westminster John Knox, 2009), 1; Michael H. Kibbe, "Present and Accommodated For: Calvin's God on Mount Sinai," *Journal of Theological Interpretation* 7, no. 1 (2013): 116; Jordan L. Steffaniak, "Bound by the Word of God: John Calvin's Religious Epistemology," *Puritan Reformed Journal* 10, no. 2 (July 2018): 135–36; John Calvin, *Institutes of the Christian Religion*, ed. John T McNeill, trans. Ford Lewis Battles (Louisville: Westminster John Knox, 2006), 1.10.2; 2.11.13; 2.16.2; 3.2.14.

25 Calvin, *Institutes of the Christian Religion*, 2.16.3.

26 Calvin, *Institutes of the Christian Religion*, 1.13.1.

is about his rejection of these classical doctrines because he claims to affirm traditional Reformed theology, including 2LCF. Johnson's claims amount to what is called *Neo-Classical Theism* and is championed by thinkers ranging from William Lane Craig to Bruce Ware to John Frame. If you are reading this, you might be a Neo-Classical Theist, and that's fine! But I think it's important to note that it is impossible to reconcile most forms of Neo-Classical Theism with 2LCF and I am skeptical that *any* version could be reconciled. And it is important to properly categorize Johnson. He claims to be defending Classical Theism, but he is really defending something else.

3.3 The Problem of Source Citation

The final problem I want to expand on is Johnson's interaction with source material. There are two related problems. First, is his handling of source material that he *does* cite. In short, by the end of the book, I found myself double checking every major citation he made because I came to distrust his handling of source material. I found him frequently pulling quotes out of context to fit his argument or not understanding what the source was intending to say. I'll give several examples to prove this. First, he quotes Robert Letham in support of his view on natural theology but Letham's context is about *atheists* attempting natural theology like Richard Dawkins and *not* Christians like Anselm, Augustine, or Thomas (22). Second, he says that Craig Carter denies "God's relatability." But he doesn't. Carter is at pains to deny "Relational Theism." This is a technical term designed to demarcate between various models of God. More than attributing a false belief to Carter this evidences a serious lack of understanding of the literature. Third, he cites Augustine, Bavinck, and Turretin as claiming God is "simple and manifold" and thus not simple in the Thomistic sense (158-159). Bavinck directly references Augustine with his claim. But familiarity with these authors and their context militates against understanding "multiplicity" as complex. For example, Bavinck follows Thomas by claiming that God is "pure essence without accidents" and "is everything he possesses."[27] Turretin similarly says that God is "free from all composition and division."[28] Finally, the quote from Augustine that Johnson relies on, if given its full context, clearly does *not* mean God is simple *and* complex. Examine for yourself: "for God it is the same thing to be as to be powerful or just or wise or anything else that can be said about his simple

---

27 Bavinck, *RD*, 2:174.
28 Turretin, *Institutes of Elenctic Theology,* 1:191.

multiplicity or multiple simplicity to signify his substance."[29] If nothing else, I think this proves that one ought to be very skeptical of his claims that any theologian "supports" his view.

The second problem related to source citation is his shocking lack of interaction with numerous important interlocutors. Certainly, he is aware of James Dolezal who is a popular Reformed Baptist and has published two books directly related to Johnson's topic—a monograph on simplicity and a trade book on the classical attributes. Yet Dolezal doesn't make an appearance. He must also know of Richard Barcellos' work on *Trinity and Creation*. Barcellos provides a lucid defense of the classical understanding of God. I'm sure he is also aware of Steven Duby's numerous books and articles that engage all the questions that Johnson asks and answers them all in traditional rather than novel ways. His recent book on *God in Himself* is dedicated to defending exactly what Johnson seeks to destroy. He must also be familiar with Tyler Wittman's work under John Webster, addressing this very problem of Thomas and the doctrine of creation. But none of these sources appear. Nor do most of the classic Thomistic resources. I even did a quick Google search on *Faith & Philosophy* and *Religious Studies*—two of the premier and most well-known journals that think about topics that Johnson is addressing (and *Faith & Philosophy* is open-access! No library subscription needed). I simply searched "Aquinas Simplicity" and in under 10 minutes had over 25 peer-reviewed articles from the top thinkers in the last 30 years interacting with these problems. None of whom Johnson interacts with. Take several examples that would be of great assistance: Katherin Rogers *The Traditional Doctrine of Divine Simplicity*, Rob Koons *Divine Persons as Relational qua-objects*, Joseph Lenow, *Shoring Up Divine Simplicity Against Modal Collapse*, William Mann *Divine Simplicity*, Eleonore Stump and Norman Kretzmann *Absolute Simplicity*, Timothy O'Connor *Simplicity and Creation*, Thomas Sullivan *Omniscience, Immutability, and the Divine Mode of Knowing*, and W. Matthews Grant *Divine Simplicity, Contingent Truths, and Extrinsic Models of Divine Knowing*. And this didn't even include me searching for things like natural theology or immutability. *Modern Theology* even had an entire issue dedicated to divine simplicity in 2019.

4. Honoring where Honor is Due

Now, despite these numerous concerns, I will commend Johnson for three

---

29 Augustine, *The Trinity,* trans. Edmund Hill (Hyde Park, NY: New City, 2015), 209.

things, though these do not overcome the problems with the book. First, he does put his finger on areas that need serious attention. It is not as if Johnson is asking *bad* questions. He simply comes to the wrong conclusion, provides bad argumentation, and is unaware of the vast literature on the topic. Second, I actually agree with some of his takes on analogical predication. I think he misunderstands a lot of what's going on there, but his basic point that there must be some point of contact, some similarity, is right. Third, I think Johnson is exactly right when he claims that "classical theism is not Thomism" and that Thomas was viewed as an innovator in his day (4). Unfortunately, Johnson goes on to misunderstand and revise much of the tradition. I think there is a great need for a more generous Classical Theism but the way forward is not to make bad arguments but to dive even deeper into the tradition.

5. Conclusion

As can be seen, I find Johnson's book to be overwhelmingly problematic. Such a claim may be an understatement. I conclude this way not only because I disagree with his conclusions but because his overall method of argumentation and representation is dreadful. Thus, Johnson does not advance the conversation forward in any meaningful sense. While I often recommend books I disagree with because they open up new ways to think about old problems or ask great questions, Johnson's book does not do this. There is nothing original that couldn't be found in a better work elsewhere. It provides no new insights, it doesn't ask new questions, it doesn't provide interaction with new sources. So, I do not recommend that anyone read this book. I recommend that those uncomfortable with Classical Theism, looking for a more moderate approach, read other resources. I recommend that those who are committed Classical Theists do the same.

Book Review:
Contemplating God with the Great Tradition: Trinitarian Classical Theism

Craig A. Carter. *Contemplating God with the Great Tradition: Recovering Trinitarian Classical Theism.* Grand Rapids: Baker Academic, 2021. 280pp. $39.99.

Reviewed by Jordan L. Steffaniak, ThM

Craig A. Carter is Research Professor of theology at Tyndale University and Theologian in residence at Westney Heights Baptist Church. In addition to *Contemplating God with the Great Tradition* Carter recently published the wildly popular first volume in this series, *Interpreting Scripture with the Great Tradition*.

The goal of this critical review is to answer the following two questions: (1) Is it worth buying and reading *Contemplating God with the Great Tradition?* (2) Are there problems with *Contemplating God with the Great Tradition?* To answer these, I will first give a brief summary before critically engaging it, since it is necessary to orient those who haven't read the work and to ensure a proper and charitable reading. The reviewer that fails to understand the goal, scope, and content of the work they are critically engaging ought to be ignored. As a note, I take "critical" in an older, more robust, sense that is not merely negative but wholly serious, examining arguments with penetrating depth without sacrificing charity because thought about God is the most serious subject matter one could encounter and any claims about him deserve such a careful posture. However, charity does not mean overlooking deficiencies. But it does require allowing the subject to speak on its own terms. I ultimately conclude that there are enough serious problems within *Contemplating God with the Great Tradition* that it is not worth buying or reading. I realize this is a bold claim given its popularity, but I think it is warranted as I intend to show.

1. Summarizing Contemplating God with the Great Tradition

Contemplating God with the Great Tradition is broken down into three parts: (1) defining trinitarian classical theism (henceforth TCT), (2) displaying the biblical roots of TCT, and (3) examining TCT in history. Carter's chief aim is to recover TCT. He suggests as much: "The purpose of this book is to establish congruence between the classical Nicene doctrine of God and the teaching of Holy Scripture" (44). He claims that TCT is the historic orthodox doctrine of God wherein modern relational theism (henceforth RT) is the opposite—modern and unorthodox—falsely worshiping an idolatrous "God" that is changed by the world rather than the God of TCT that is the "simple, immutable, eternal, self-existent First Cause of the cosmos" (16). Carter is insistent that TCT has been the universal opinion of thinkers from the fourth to eighteenth centuries with no variation (282).

Carter begins his retrieval attempt in chapter 1, finding the task necessary because modern theology has unwittingly imbibed metaphysical assumptions contrary to what is required by the fourth century Fathers and the Nicene Creed. Therefore, modern theology followed to its logical conclusion is a reversion to pagan mythology rather than true Christianity. Some of these faulty modern assumptions are noted by Carter from the beginning, such as the tension between divine immutability and divine impassibility. Before the nineteenth century Carter says that "virtually no Christian theologian thought that there was any tension" between these two doctrines (15). These modern problems arise primarily due to three problematic trends in most of modern theology: (1) it discusses the attributes separately from the Trinity (2) it is too impatient with mystery and punts to contradictions (3) it ignores history (22). Thus, the eighteenth and nineteenth centuries' steep decline from TCT to RT is due in large part to its faulty modern exegetical approach. If TCT is to be recovered, premodern exegesis must be recovered (36).

Carter spends the entire second chapter attempting to define TCT via 25 theses. These range from broad claims affirmed by those that would reject TCT such as Christian theology being about God and derived from Scripture to more contentious theses such as God is pure act (51, 52, 65). Thesis 11 is the one that does much of the heavy lifting in Carter's thinking throughout the book. It claims that *"God is transcendent, which means that he is not a being within the universe but the sovereign Lord of all that exists"* (67). Herein one also finds Carter's central claim regarding the *metaphysics* of Nicaea. He describes it as a "sacramental ontology" or Christian Platonism (55).

Carter then moves in part two to three chapters engaging theological methodology and scriptural exegesis, focused on Isaiah 40–48. An important part of this section is to understand the context of Isaiah and the nature of revelation. Carter rejects modern biblical trends that ignore the broader *canonical* and *divine* context and the reliability of the text. Scripture is not a mere human creation but one superintended by God and thus is coherent and relevant for all time (87). The historical critical method is a dead-end method. Carter spends a significant amount of real estate critiquing those who find predictive prophecy impossible. He also suggests that TCT is mutually illuminating to Isaiah—it arises naturally and allows deeper understanding (86). For him, anything besides TCT is a departure from the plain sense and a reversion to pagan mythology (86). The second important part of this section is to show how Isaiah confirms Thesis 11. He concludes as follows:

> Isaiah's belief in a transcendent Creator rules out the possibility of any sort of pantheism, panentheism, theistic personalism, or theistic mutualism, because all of these doctrines view the divine as part of the cosmos rather than before and above the cosmos (183).

So, Carter suggests that Isaiah's understanding of God as transcendent Creator means TCT is *necessarily* true. Every other model of God is ruled out from the start since none can affirm God as transcendent Creator.

The third section engages more of the tradition in chapter 7 from Justin Martyr to Irenaeus to Athanasius. Here he shows how these thinkers all promote the same Isaianic themes of transcendence, sovereignty, and monotheism. Chapter 8 is devoted to the doctrine of *creatio ex nihilo* since it is at the heart of TCT and is key to recovering it (238). Carter concludes in chapter 9 by evaluating several modern theologians in light of the assumption of TCT. Pannenberg and Moltmann are key targets herein.

2. Critical Engagement: The Negatives

Given this rough summary, my intent is to critically interact with Carter's work, thereby highlighting serious deficiencies. Afterward I do intend to highlight some areas of agreement. Afterall, I think Carter and I are similar in many ways. For example, I critique Carter as a *fellow Classical Theist*. I have drunk deeply from the medieval and Reformed tradition and find it beautiful, rich, resourceful, and summarized well in the Second London Baptist Confession of Faith Cahpter 2. Moreover, I'm more than simply a Classical Theist in name. I have also researched and published in defense of it. My ThM thesis was a defense of the method and metaphysics of Classical Theism, retrieving from Augustine and Thomas Aquinas. My PhD dissertation assumes Conciliar Christology as basic. I critique as one convinced of Classical Theism and one actively defending it.

I begin with the areas of deficiency. The first problem is one that I have noted in the past regarding Carter—a tendency to be so polemical that careful critical engagement is missed. For example, throughout the book Carter loads terms like "modern" with incredible amounts of negative baggage without proving his assumptions. This tactic in popular contemporary thought is often called poisoning the well. Essentially, Carter attempts to influence the reader to have a negative perception of his opponents before ever offering them the opportunity to speak for themselves. Let's begin with an easy one that is close to home for me. At the end of chapter 8 Carter flippantly mentions how theistic personalism is embraced by "many analytic philosophers today" (268). Maybe this is true. Maybe it isn't. But no one would be able to determine if it is since Carter cites no one. Much less does he explain what he means by analytic philosopher. This is a problem throughout the book. Oftentimes I am left wondering if I should trust Carter's rendition of his opponents given that he rarely cites them or presents the best form of their argument. Carter shows little interest in understanding the nuance of others thought. To my knowledge (two fairly thorough readings of the book thus far), one of the only citations he has of an analytic philosopher besides Ed Feser is Richard Swinburne. However, he cites him second hand through Brian Davies and evidences his ignorance of Swinburne given that Swinburne has continually amended his views over time (17). I do not have confidence that Carter has actually read these "analytic philosophers" that he so quickly dismisses.

The most concerning trend in this book relates to the terminology of *modern*. Carter belabors his disdain for all things modern, especially *modern metaphysics*. But it is never clear what modern metaphysics means, who accepts modern metaphysics, and why it is so bad to accept modern metaphysics. However, throughout Carter's work you can find breadcrumbs to what he means by modern metaphysics. Carter suggests it is "very different," "incompatible," and "contradictory" with Nicaea (29). He claims it wants to fit the Bible into a naturalistic framework (237). Central to it is a loss of divine transcendence (144). It thinks that God is part of the universe (239). It is revisionary (205, 217). It is uncritical of its metaphysical assumptions (50). It considers the findings of physics and biology to be "unchallengeable" (241). The most robust summary is given in a negative fashion. Modern metaphysics rejects a transcendent God, an objectively existing telos in nature, metaphysical realism by which things have natures, and a linear concept of history (172). Carter elsewhere suggests that "Modern metaphysics is thus better understood as a rejection of metaphysics insofar as it is actually a reversion to ancient mythology" (120).

Given this smattering of examples, it is quite clear that Carter hasn't read contemporary *modern* metaphysicians—much less *metaphysics*, modern, scholastic, or otherwise. If I read this sample of what modern metaphysics apparently means to a group of modern metaphysicians they would find it unrecognizable. Indeed, modern metaphysics is in an unbelievably wide term that includes those who would affirm TCT and those who wouldn't. Does Carter mean to implicate those like William Lane Craig, John Peckham, Richard Swinburne, R.T. Mullins, or Jay Wesley Richards who *do* attempt to revise TCT at points? Or does he intend to reject the modern neo-Aristotelian metaphysical work from those such as Rob Koons, Alex Pruss, or Ross Inman? Or does he intend to reject the list of modern metaphysicians attempting to retrieve from the tradition such as Eleonore Stump, Jeff Brower, Tim Pawl, Brian Leftow, Ross Inman, Ed Feser, or Greg Welty? I'm sure he wants to reject the initial group, but by his pejorative labeling he actually implicates all of them. But let's say Carter actually intends to refer to atheistic naturalism and would give a free pass to these thinkers. Does he then mean to take aim at those like Thomas Nagel who explicitly affirm metaphysical realism and an objectively existing telos in nature? I have no idea if he would—but that's because he either hasn't read them or hasn't understood them. If he had read them and understood them, surely he would have taken the time to include their examples in an academic work devoted to critiquing their thought. But he doesn't. Much less does he realize that what he pejoratively calls modern metaphysics is ignorant of modern metaphysics. He could begin by reading Alvin Plantinga's *Advice to Christian Philosophers* to notice the wide disparity between what he calls modern and what actually is modern. Or a single reading of something as simple as *Contemporary Debates in Metaphysics* would cure most of these blunders. But I fear metaphysics is more of a power word for him than one with definable content. If you shout it loud enough, long enough, and confident enough, dissenters will assume you are correct. Don't get me wrong—there is a place for polemics. But the place for polemics is situated within a deep engagement with one's opponents, evidencing a grasp of their thinking and arguments. Carter, unfortunately, does not evidence either a grasp of his opponents. Even more, ironic as it may sound, Carter relies on his definition of divine *transcendence* to defend TCT but terms such as transcendence and *immanence* are actually modern terms that became popular during, you guessed it, the Enlightenment. It is striking for Carter to base his entire argument for TCT on modern concepts and yet vilify it at the same time.

The second problem is a striking level of ambiguity and misunderstanding of TCT itself at various points. One would think that someone attempting to recover TCT would have a solid grasp of the core set of doctrines enshrined in TCT. But Carter does not evidence either a deep familiarity with the tradition or an understanding of some of the key doctrines. One example is his mistake regarding mercy and wrath as divine attributes (25, 75). He categorizes these explicitly as attributes alongside love and justice, etc. However, this is not the way the classical tradition has spoken regarding these. Mercy and wrath are not *properly* attributes of God. They are what Turretin calls an *egress* or *exercise* of his attributes. This is the distinction between theology and economy (a distinction that Carter actually references elsewhere himself [233]). A brief survey of the Reformed tradition reveals a consistent understanding along Turretin's lines. For example, Petrus van Mastricht argues that mercy is "nothing but grace toward the miserable"—it is a subset of grace which is a subset of goodness.[1] Elsewhere he explains that wrath is "nothing but his avenging justice."[2] Herman Bavinck and William Shedd concur, viewing mercy as God's goodness shown to those in misery.[3] Wrath is part of God's retributive justice. As Shedd explains, "in a sinless world, there would be no place for its exercise, and it would be comparatively an unimportant aspect of the general attribute of justice."[4] Therefore, mercy and wrath are properly not attributes but an egress of God's perfect goodness and justice.

Another example relates to immutability and impassibility. Carter defines immutability as God "not either receiving or losing life as all creatures are doing" (65). But such a definition is shockingly thin compared to the classical tradition. In fact, such a definition is so thin that it would likely allow most RT's to affirm it. Elsewhere Carter notes that "the doctrines of immutability and impassibility say that God does not change in his essence" (25). But again, this displays ignorance of the tradition. Immutability is much more than changelessness in essence—it is an *impossibility* of change in both nature *and* will. It is a doctrine wherein God neither undergoes affective change nor feels the actions of creatures. Lest one think this is either out of step with the tradition or a minor point, consider the voluminous support for such a definition. Turretin, van Mastricht, Bavinck, Shedd, and Muller all provide this robust understanding of immutability.[5] And impassibility

1   Peter van Mastricht, *Theoretical-Practical Theology*, ed. Joel R. Beeke, trans. Todd M. Rester (Grand Rapids: Reformation Heritage Books, 2018), 2:345.
2   Mastricht, 2:355.
3   Herman Bavinck, *Reformed Dogmatics*, ed. John Bolt, trans. John Vriend (Grand Rapids: Baker Academic, 2003), 2:213; William G. T. Shedd, *Dogmatic Theology*, 3rd ed (Phillipsburg, N.J: P&R, 2003), 306.
4   Shedd, *Dogmatic Theology*, 295.
5   Francis Turretin, *Institutes of Elenctic Theology*, ed. James T. Dennison, trans. George Musgrave Giger (Phillipsburg, NJ: P&R, 1994), 1:204; Mastricht, *Theoretical-Practical Theology*, 2:157; Bavinck, *RD*, 2:153-154; Shedd, *Dogmatic Theology*, 284; Richard A. Muller, *Post-Reformation*

is more than not receiving or losing life but an inability to be *acted upon* altogether. Carter's definitions leave me scratching my head as to where he is retrieving TCT from. To be fair, I imagine Carter would affirm these definitions if presented to him—however his writing doesn't evidence a deep understanding of them. For a book with the title *Contemplating God with the Great Tradition,* I think it would have benefited from more time immersed in the *Great Tradition* to remedy some of these sorts of errors.

A third problem relates to the overall level of argumentation in the book. Carter frequently misunderstands how logical deductions work. Take three examples. First, Carter explains that "when relational theism affirms two-way relations of causality and change between God and creatures, it eliminates the uniqueness of God and brings him down to the level of a creature" (19-20). But this statement isn't a logical inference—it is an assertion. Assertions must be proved by argumentation. Carter doesn't provide this. Maybe it is true that two-way relations eliminate God's uniqueness. But nowhere is it clear why it does so. Nowhere are we sure what these "relations" metaphysically amount to either. Maybe they are innocuous. If Carter was familiar with the metaphysical debates over the status of relations—either in scholastic or modern thinking—he would know this would require further clarification. But we aren't given the details. The argument isn't explained—it is merely asserted. Take a second example where Carter attempts to prove that God is pure act:

> If there is a First Cause, that First Cause must be pure actuality in order to be uncaused. Therefore, God must be pure act. This metaphysical proof is not a matter of probability; nor is it a matter of arguing that the universe must have had a cause to get it started. It is a logical deduction that is certain, not merely probable (60).

Now, as a Classical Theist myself, I'd be delighted to find an argument for Classical Theism that originated in the basic fact that God is Creator such as Carter has attempted to construct here. But again, Carter makes assertions without argumentation. The key undefended premise is that the First Cause must be pure actuality in order to be uncaused. Nowhere is this proven—it is asserted. But mere assertions do not substitute for rigorous argumentation. They may win debates with those unfamiliar with the terminology, but they will not win converts among those with understanding. If the goal of Carter's book is to self-congratulate those that already affirm TCT, this form of thinking may work, but if he intends to persuade those that either are unsure or disagree, this will do more harm than anything. Finally, take Carter's most important claim in the book: "a transcendent Creator rules out the possibility of any sort of pantheism, panentheism, theistic personalism, or theistic mutualism, because all of these doctrines view the divine as part of the cosmos rather than before and above the cosmos" (183). Unfortunately, there are several problems with this argument. First, it is unclear what transcendence means besides the Creator-creature distinction which many RT's explicitly affirm. They would explicitly affirm transcendence and the Creator-creature distinction but reject the conclusion that Carter comes to from this initial premise. It doesn't necessarily follow from transcendence that RT is false or that RT views God as part of the cosmos. If Carter wants to establish this claim, he needs to provide significantly more premises. As this argument stands, the RT can affirm all the same premises that Carter does and yet reject the conclusion. This is an invalid argument. Carter must either provide an argument wherein RT affirms all of the premises and is left with the conclusion that God is part of the cosmos or an argument wherein they reject a premise that is required for the conclusion that God is transcendent. Second, Carter seems to beg the question with his conclusion by assuming that the only way for God to be "before and above" the cosmos is by adopting TCT. But Carter doesn't explain why this is the case. He merely assumes that only TCT can make sense of it.

A fourth problem is his preoccupation with the Hellenization thesis (the thesis that the early Christians were unduly influenced by pagan Greek metaphysics and thus TCT should be rejected for its contamination). Throughout the book Carter continually suggests that modern thinkers reject TCT because of it (49, 85, 208-209, 272). But as has been shown throughout my critique, Carter doesn't cite examples of modern Christians who are actually using the thesis to reject TCT. Sure, the creator of the foolish thesis in von Harnack is one, but what about all of the contemporary RT's? I don't know of any that are depending on the Hellenization thesis for their claims. Carter is stuck in the nineteenth century with his critiques. Now, it's fine to critique the incredibly ignorant claims of von Harnack and the like on this topic—but if we intend to critique an entire group that is diverse and actually rejects the Hellenization thesis, this claim will only give more reasons to ignore TCT.

A fifth problem, though not unique to Carter, is his misunderstanding of the equivocal, analogical, univocal language debate. Consider what Carter says: "to speak of God in a *univocal* way would mean that every aspect of what "father" means in human terms would apply to God....The only way our language about God can be meaningful without reducing God to the level of a creature, then, is if it is *analogical*" (69). The problem here is that this definition of univocal language is not true. Univocal language does not require that *every* aspect of the term correspond—it only requires that there is a univocal core of meaning—which is actually required for analogical language to be coherent. If univocity requires every aspect to be identical then it is an absurd thesis that doesn't even apply to everyday objects. There is always something that differs, no matter how small, between objects.

A sixth problem is overly frequent misunderstanding or misrepresentation of his opponent's beliefs. As has been seen throughout my critique, Carter lacks wide citations of his opponents and often makes entailments that do not follow. But Carter also makes *completely false* statements about some of his opponents. For example, he says that "In modern relational theism, the simplicity and aseity of God are denied, and God is seen as existing in a relationship to creation similar to the kind of relationship one creature has with another" (19). *This is unequivocally false.* RT has some of the most serious defenders of aseity to date. William Lane Craig is a chief example. He has an entire book devoted to defending divine aseity—*God Over All*. Unless Carter is willing to say that William Lane Craig, despite attempting to defend divine aseity, is actually rejecting it, I see no other way to understand Carter's claim than either ignorance of the wider literature or blatant lying. I take it that the former is the case. But if Carter is genuinely this ignorant of the wider literature on the doctrine of God, I do not think he is competent enough to be publishing work in the area. Such claims may be understandable by a Master's student who is only beginning to wrestle with an area but should never be acceptable in a published work. Take another example. Carter says that modern theology thinks that God should be "easily understandable" (28). I know of no RT that thinks this and Carter doesn't cite anyone who suggests as much. These are unacceptable assertions to an author's opponents. Even when our opponents are completely wrong, they deserve a careful hearing. James exhorts us to listen before we speak. Assertions and criticisms ought to be made—but they should be made with proper documentation.

A final problem relates to the overall content and goal of the book. Consider how important it was for Carter to include the Trinity within Classical Theism (hence TCT and not CT). Part of the problem of modern theologians is considering the attributes apart from the Trinity. However, Carter seems to do just this. There is no clear exposition of the Trinity nor is there a connection made between the attributes and God's triune nature. Carter's actual product would be better understood as a promotion of a robust divine transcendence and not TCT.

3. Critical Engagement: The Positives

Now, Carter's book isn't all negative. There are some strengths—it's not a complete black hole. First, Carter is absolutely right about our need to think critically about our metaphysical presuppositions (48). This is something he hammers home in his first book, *Interpreting Scripture with the Great Tradition.* It is impossible to leave our presuppositions at home when interpreting Scripture. No one has a "me and my Bible only" theology. Anyone that attempts to suggest otherwise is dead wrong. Second, I think Carter's actual exegesis of Isaiah 40-48 is great. He handles the problematic aspects of many modern biblical scholars well. His critiques of those who reject predictive prophecy, those who disjoint the narrative of Isaiah, and those who are beholden to the historical critical method are excellent. He unearths the key insights from the text: transcendence and sovereignty. Had this book been solely dedicated to his exposition of Isaiah 40-48 I would have no problem commending it as a great resource. Third, Carter is a talented writer. Whether one agrees with Carter or not—they can recognize his gift for writing. It is smooth and powerful. It is never a labor to read but always a treat. It is this writing style that has made him such a powerful popularizer of TCT. People of all walks can understand him. A fourth aspect I really appreciate is his understanding that the patristics were not under some Greek spell wherein they simply imbibed the metaphysical assumptions of the day without critical engagement. For example, he says, "The fathers were determined to integrate what was salvageable from Greek philosophy into a Christian worldview built on the basis of biblical exegesis because they wanted to assimilate all human culture into a biblical framework" (205). It is this type of work that I wholeheartedly support. My only wish is that such opportunities would be extended beyond the fourth century. Christians in every age ought to want to assimilate all human culture into a biblical framework. The Spirit of God is not frozen in 381. There are other aspects that I found beneficial throughout the book but given the goal of this review as primarily a critical interaction, I leave them to the reader to discern for themselves.

4. Conclusion

So, is it worth buying and reading *Contemplating God with the Great Tradition?* At the outset of this review I said no. But a better answer might be: Maybe, but *probably* not. If you are an undergraduate or graduate student wanting to understand the classical doctrine of God, as much as I hate to say it, this isn't the book for you. If you are an academic researcher on the doctrine of God, you might need to read it. But even then, it's not serious scholarship. Carter's work is oftentimes more akin to Classical Theism propaganda than it is a defense or retrieval. While this may be okay for the reader who is already convinced of TCT, it is detrimental to those seeking understanding or considering changing their minds. But while I suggest that it is not worth reading, I wish it was. I want more measured, serious, erudite, and fair, retrieval of Classical Theism. I want more theological retrieval that is deep in history but conversant and aware of modernity. I want more that persuasively engages with opponents. If TCT is to survive the continued assault on its central doctrines, we need more retrieval. Sadly, while I love and share Carter's goal of retrieving the Great Tradition, I think this book fails to do so. I take no pleasure in providing such a critical review. The business of critiquing bad books is not one I delight in. However, a robust defense of the Confession and a commitment to *critical* thinking requires serious examination which has resulted in what I think is a failed book. And herein is the great danger of Carter's work. It is incredibly popular. And while I am a Classical Theist, blatant misrepresentations like Carter's will make it even more difficult to fight against the trend of rejecting TCT. Unserious popularizing of ideas like this most often bears bad fruit in time because those caught up in the movement do not have the proper roots. But there is good news. There are other resources that can provide a serious engagement with the tradition. If one is partial to more polemical and blunt writing, James Dolezal is a great example of a serious and well-researched defense. There are other more measured defenses from those like Tim Pawl and Katherin Rogers which ought to be engaged. There are also other excellent recent works by Reformed Baptists who confess the Second London Baptist Confession of Faith like Richard Barcellos and Sam Renihan. But of course, I would be remiss if I didn't simply recommend the great Reformed systematicians themselves. There is a reason people continue to read Calvin, Turretin, Bavinck, and the like. The Great Tradition is far greater than Carter exemplifies in this book. The challenges of RT are not new to the twenty-first century. So, despite the deep and damning flaws found in Carter's work, I do hope that it functions as a catalyst for more reflective study on the merits of Classical Theism.

Book Review:
The Mission of God: A Manifesto of Hope for Society

Boot, Joseph. *The Mission of God: A Manifesto of Hope for Society*. London: Wilberforce Publications, 2016. Second edition. 673 pp. Softcover. ISBN 9780957572560. $22.77.

Reviewed by Tom Musseti, ThM

Joe Boot earned his doctorate from Whitefield Theological Seminary and is the author of numerous books on apologetics and cultural engagement.[1] He is the founder of the Ezra Institute for Contemporary Christianity and founding pastor of Westminster Chapel in Toronto, Ontario. His work, *The Mission of God* (TMG), is something of a magnum opus and has garnered much attention and a favorable reception since its publication. TMG has cast a large shadow in Ontario and beyond, leading many pastors and congregants to accept its theonomic conclusions and adopt its postmillennialism. I began reading TMG when my former pastor began his move towards theonomic postmillennialism, commenting that he believed Boot to be the foremost theologian of our day. From the perspective of this reviewer who resides in Southern Ontario, Boot's ideas in TMG need to be critically appraised from a biblical perspective. Since its publication in 2014, no substantial review of the work (as far as I am aware) has been published. The present review will succinctly summarize the main tenets of TMG followed by a critical evaluation of what I take to be serious deficiencies.

1. Summary

The book is divided into two parts, totaling thirteen chapters. Most chapters have a problem-solution structure: Boot presents a cultural issue then provides a biblical solution to the issue. The foundational, catch-all solution to present-day global crises is found in a recovery of biblical law for society. Such recovery is deeply embedded in the hope for a prosperous and free

---

1   Whitefield is an unaccredited school in Lakeland, Florida

future. For Boot, the use and application of biblical law has tremendous historical precedence in Western civilization, particularly during the Puritan era. Evidently, the West now suffers from countless evils, and the rise of godlessness can be attributed to an abandonment of the use of God's law.

The modern church plays a role in this abandonment. Boot observes that the church has dichotomized law and gospel, leading to a decline of biblical authority, especially the authority of the Old Testament (99). This dichotomizing can be seen in the concept of two kingdoms. He understands two-kingdom theology as a sort of cultural retreatism, an excuse for Christians to eschew involvement outside the walls of the church, thus driving an unnecessary wedge between Christians as the church and Christians in the world (381). When the church adopts any measure of natural law, according to Boot, this becomes a dire disservice, for natural law is a futile enterprise that cannot prescribe moral imperatives (261-269). As biblical law is removed from the entire scope of human affairs, decay ensues. Consequently, within judicial systems, a rise in "cheap grace" (as Boot calls it) seems almost ubiquitous, undermining true justice by softening punishments for crimes (296-299). This is also evident in education. Boot heavily questions the idea of neutrality in education, arguing that state-sanctioned pedagogy leads to deleterious consequences in society, precisely because it is ideological and pagan (442-451).

Arguably, the solution to all social evils is a recovery of biblical law *in toto* (25). Boot alleges that Chalcedon was the foundation of Western civilization and that the current task of the church is to see the state converted and faithfully submitting to Christ (154). The relevance of God's law for society continues to be abiding. As leaders of the past established societies based on the pattern of Old Testament Israel, so too should the leaders of today seek to build a theocratic society (289). Only then will we see an increase in social, religious, and economic freedoms. The concluding mandate of the book is captured in a single statement: "We are therefore called unequivocally to spread the culture of Christ to all creation" (398).

2. Analysis

Given its length, TMG is undoubtedly a work of deep commitment and perseverance. The book exhibits the labor of a passionate Christian, who is deeply concerned about the state of the church. Boot's observations about the decline of society and the turn away from the Scriptures are noteworthy, precisely because many churches have tended to go with the flow of secular ideologies. The imminent dangers of the public education system in Canada, with its emphases on counter-biblical sexuality and issues of identity are prominently highlighted. This is good and important, and the church would do well to keep these matters close to heart.

A key strength of TMG is the number of references to present-day issues. Boot provides numerous examples of how the English-speaking nations are abandoning biblical law in favor of "cheap grace," which substitutes justice for ideology. Even where there is disagreement between Christians on sources of law (nature or God), there can be no question that without a transcendent lawgiver all laws are necessarily fluid. Boot rightly underscores the inescapability of God in the quest for justice.

While the book has its merits, its shortcomings are rather prominent. Chief among them is the work's sluggish exegesis. Before diving into the specifics, it is important to note that the work lacks clear definitions. The concept of biblical law is sometimes used as "Mosaic law" and sometimes used as "law of Christ," thus creating ambiguity. This lack of clarity also shows up in Boot's engagement with the idea of education. We are often given examples, but the ambiguating factor emerges as readers cannot discern whether he is speaking of particular instances of an educational system or every educational system in the West—after all, these systems are largely dependent on the subcommunities within which they function. Puritanism, which features prominently in the work, also suffers from a lack of definition, as does "dualism," a term historically loaded with heavy philosophical freight. Insofar as this review attempts to give TMG a fair hearing, the scarcity of clarity in defining terms often makes the task challenging. We turn now to some critical observations.

In the course of showing that any division between law and gospel in the NT is dualistic and artificial, Boot appeals to Titus 2:11-15 for support. He points to this Pauline text to show that the bifurcation of "the Old Testament as law and the New Testament as gospel" is artificial and false. The conclusion drawn is that "Paul makes plain here the unity of Old and New Testaments, showing that the grace of God is manifest in Christ's work of redeeming us from 'lawlessness,' purifying us for his own possession" (98).

Three observations can be made. First, the passage is silent on the law. The only occurrence of "law" in Titus is at 3:9, where Paul enjoins Titus to avoid quarrels about the law. Second, the passage highlights the present age as one lived in anticipation of the second coming, not an earthly Christian golden age. The grace that appeared (2:11) trains believers *to renounce* spiritual vices and *to live* "self-controlled, upright, and godly lives in the *present age*" (v. 12).

Boot fails to take stock of something very clear and possibly antithetical to his theological position: the present age is characterized by "waiting for our blessed hope, the appearing of the glory of our great God and Saviour Jesus Christ." Contextually and theologically, Jesus Christ's appearing is physical and serves as the necessary and sufficient source of our hope in the present age. Boot does not parse out the meaning of "hope" nor his understanding of "appearing." Furthermore, his exclusive focus on the *present* aspect of the passage is at the expense of the *future* aspect of the passage, and this leads to a dilemma. Either take the future blessed hope and the appearing of Jesus as the millennial golden age, thus spiritualizing the second coming ("appearing") of Jesus Christ *or* accept that waiting for the second coming is the motivating factor to live godly lives, thereby undermining the chief postmillennial thesis of TMG. Since the goal of TMG is to reform society, Boot's reading of Titus 2:11-15 appears to suggest that Christ's second coming will not be physical but, rather, spiritual. If I understand Boot correctly, and if the subtitle of TMG serves as an indicator (*A Manifesto of Hope for Society*), the idea of hope is grounded in law-keeping, not in the future anticipation of Christ's bodily return. Third, and perhaps most embarrassingly for Boot, is his unambiguous misreading of the passage. He observes that the redeemed people "are zealous for the good works" (v. 14). Certainly, he is correct, for the text says exactly that. But his full observation reads, "are zealous for the good works and the life of self-control *prescribed in God's law*" (99, emphasis mine). The mention of "law" was introduced in a rather back-door manner, manipulating the passage so that it appears to support Boot's position.

Another example turns up in the chapter on Christian education. While Boot aptly shows the weaknesses of public education as a system built on increasingly godless ideologies, his attempt to defend a biblical mandate of education is short of successful. Where biblical references are found, these are not explained and can often be interpreted in other ways. His argument in defense of a Christian curriculum is largely dependent on one text: Matthew 28:18-20. This is the only text Boot unpacks, claiming that the authority given to Christ is now translated into a mandate to educate (452).

I suggest this is a misreading of the text and an example of eisegesis. The Great Commission mandate is to make disciples of all nations. This is the only imperative in the passage. The way disciples are made is through baptizing and teaching. Presumably, the goal of the commission is to make believers (i.e., disciples) through the proclamation of the gospel, which consequently leads to the act of baptism and the work of teaching. But Boot understands this differently, or, minimally, he sees something else.

His understanding is that "teaching" includes a mandate to formally educate from a biblical worldview by establishing Christian curricula. In other words, the Great Commission's aspect of teaching includes both spiritual matters and, among other subjects, biology. However, there is nothing in the context of the passage to buttress such an imperative. At best, Boot's conclusion is a possible implication, but he failed even to make an argument for this possibility—that is, the implication was assumed.

Moreover, Boot points to Matthew 18:6-7, claiming that false education of children is something Jesus condemns. Of course, Boot rightly acknowledges that the text is referring to believers, and that "children," in the context, refers to Christ's regenerate followers. Nonetheless, he claims, "it seems clear that he [i.e., Jesus] specifically has vulnerable children in mind when he brings a child into their midst," concluding that subjecting children to non-Christian curricula is tantamount to "laying a serious stumbling block in front of our children" (454). Whether this was part of the original intent of Matthew, the reader can decide.

Boot suggests, "[a] full-orbed [i.e., inclusive of all subject matters] Christian education is the logical outworking of biblical faith in obedience to the command to raise our children in the fear and admonition of the Lord" (429). This claim garnered the most biblical support, though only by way of parenthetical references (that is to say, no exegesis). The four passages are Exodus 13:2; 34:19; Psalm 24:1-2; 127:3. I encourage readers to look up these references and decide for themselves whether they support his claim or whether they are simple proof-texts.

An important feature of TMG's thesis is that the whole earth is part of the mission of God. This goes beyond the church and includes a call to influence institutions and care for the environment. This is referred to as "the cultural mandate" (71-75). This cultural mandate, explains Boot, includes three land grants. The first land grant was Eden, which was subsequently lost. The second was Canaan. This land too was lost through exile. The third is the present land grant of the whole earth to believers. This land grant, according to Boot, "is made clear in Romans 4:13, Ephesians 6:3, Mark 10:29-30, and Matthew 5:5; 28:18-20" (73). However, even a preliminary reading of these passages indicates that none of them can plausibly support the conclusion that the earth is a land grant to believers—all are disconnected proof-texts.

In addition to the general engagement with texts of Scripture, some arguments tend to rest on dubious lexical grounds. Boot draws conclusions about the verb *plēroō* from lexicographical evidence, but he does not cite any lexicon and does not engage with the verb in any context where it occurs.

Yet he confidently concludes that *plēroō* implies that Christ has "come to implement and put into force his law" (96). Likewise, in arguing for the believer's purpose "to discipline and organize nations into covenant-obeying peoples," Boot claims that the call to discipline is contained in the Great Commission's mandate to "teach." This, he suggests, is taken from the fact that "the word *teach* in the Greek language *(mathatos)* means literally 'disciple'" (376, emphasis original). However, this is a very simplistic approach to lexicography. Words mean something in the *context* in which they are used. Perhaps most challenging to Boot is the embarrassing fact that *mathatos* never occurs in the NT in any form whatsoever, whether it be its lexical (dictionary) form or derived forms. (The transliterated word *mathatos* does occur in non-NT literature; perhaps he meant μαθητής *[mathētēs]*).

The book also demonstrates a great inability by the author to provide relevant evidence to buttress positions and is woefully lacking in primary sources, being largely dependent on secondary works. Boot's analysis of justice illustrates this well. Several pages are dedicated to refuting Tim Keller. However, no other author is cited—Keller is the sole punching bag. Boot also discusses and critiques the work of Gustavo Gutierrez, but never quotes him directly. The same applies to his engagement with Ronald Sider. Sider apparently manipulates the Exodus story in the attempt to draw out a sort of liberation theology, and his "interpretation strains all credibility" (228). Likewise, in the engagement with Meredith Kline's "intrusion ethics," Boot concludes that Kline's eschatology is "problematic" and "convincingly refuted by Greg Bahnsen" (321–322). Kline is not referenced anywhere in the discussion.

Though many more examples can be proffered as evidence of the book's poor research methods, a final illustration is in order. One of the arguments in favor of a biblical education mandate emerges from an observation of early Jewish history. Boot explains that synagogues in the first century were places where parents sent their children to learn the Scripture and other subjects. This sort of education was made compulsory. Children studied, among other things, the Mishnah and the Talmud (426). On top of providing no historical source for these claims, Boot is grossly anachronistic. The Talmud, a monumental expansion of and commentary on the Mishnah did not exist until several centuries after the destruction of the temple. Even the Mishnah was not codified until the third century A.D., and its oral existence in the first century is a matter of significant debate.

Besides lacking primary source evidence, the work appears to have significant theological deficiencies. Perhaps most evident is a manifestly over-realized eschatology. Throughout the work, Boot refers to past societies in the West, drawing a proportionality relationship between adherence to biblical law and prosperity. The book makes little to no mention of a future kingdom after the second coming of Christ and puts forth no effort to distinguish between the heavenly and earthly, a distinction so prominent throughout the Scriptures. What is more, OT promises about land, for example, are reappropriated and applied *a priori* to the church as a physical organism— that is to say, the promises are interpreted literally, such that the kingdom of God becomes a matter of quantification. This point is clearly manifested in the book's examination of the parable of the mustard seed. Boot likens the *Christian states of being* to the mustard seed, which "grows and creates, as it has done wherever it has been in history, a type of civilization" (398). The kingdom of God's *telos* is strictly earthly and, as Boot seems to suggest, will come to full fruition before the second coming of Jesus. Practically, then, if this understanding of the kingdom is applied to Christianity in, say, present-day China, the conclusion must be that the kingdom there is rather weak.

In relation to the general understanding of the kingdom, Boot's discussion of prosperity also hints at an over-realized eschatology. He claims that a poverty-free and debt-free society can happen, if and only if God's law is obeyed. There are no biblical references in the argument, only a partial quotation from James 1:25 (251). Boot's argument is simple: following God's law will lead to the eradication of poverty and debt. No space is even considered for an engagement with Jesus' words in Matthew 26:11. The troublesome aspect of this claim is that it reveals a fundamental misunderstanding of eschatology. While there is a day coming when all tears will be wiped away, and poverty will effectively be non-existent, that day will follow the second coming of Christ. Contrary to this, Boot seems to think that a poverty-free society can be realized on this side of eternity.

Further to this point, the issue of prosperity is rather important. While the New Testament seems to be silent with respect to physical blessing as a consequence of obedience, the Old Testament is quite unequivocal in expressing that reality. Surely, we must ask why the NT is silent. But Boot does not engage that question. Rather, he assumes the OT teaching, endorsing a perspective quite similar to the prosperity gospel—if a faithful farmer is experiencing a bad season, it may likely be because of his disobedience. Thus, if we "want to see human flourishing in the land and blessing on our agriculture, cattle, wilderness and animal kingdoms," notes Boot, "we must obey God's law" (251). Boot espouses salvation by faith alone; however, it seems that he is advancing an argument for blessing based on works, rather than faith, and that membership in the kingdom requires law-keeping, a perspective quite like covenantal nomism.

Another point of contention is Boot's engagement with Philippians 3:21. He maintains that this verse supports the theonomic, postmillennial claim that Christ is to be King of the nations. Of course, Boot's understanding is that Christ will be king of all nations as a king who is not physically present. Christ will rule the earth, such that all will submit to him before his second coming. But Philippians 3:21 can hardly support this view—unless, of course, one takes the verse out of context. Boot only looks at the second part of the verse: "by the power that enables him [i.e. Jesus] even to subject all things to himself." Is this a subjection in the present age or in the age to come? Here's the verse in its context: "But our citizenship is in heaven, and from it we await a Savior, the Lord Jesus Christ, who will transform our lowly body to be like his glorious body, by the power that enables him even to subject all things to himself" (vv. 20-21). The context makes the time of Christ's subjection of all things to himself either inconclusive or in the future age, when the awaited Savior appears, and we receive our glorified bodies. Most certainly, then, the verse cannot be adduced as evidence in favor of a postmillennial global Christian dominion.

Perhaps the most questionable feature of TMG is the general approach to biblical law. Historical examples of biblical law as a basis of government far outweigh any discussion from the Scripture. In developing his position on the source of law (God or nature), Boot rejects natural theology and natural law, arguing that it is a form of self-law, which stands in absolute opposition to God's law (261-267). He does not engage with any position that defends natural theology/law (with the possible exception of one article by Michael Horton on two-kingdom theology), and no latitude is given for the role of natural law at all. Thomistic thought is rejected *a priori* as pagan ideology (265). Only four Bible references are given to counter natural law: Romans 1:24; 1:29-32; 2; 2:14-15. But these merely occur parenthetically, and no exegetical argument is put forward. Furthermore, in approaching the question of Paul and the law, again, there is no exegetical engagement (100-102). The best one finds are sporadic, free-standing verses. No discussion of Paul's understanding of the law in Galatians is found anywhere in the book—all Galatians references related to the law appear in TMG in only one paragraph. What is more, Boot's arguments against law-gospel dualism seems to be at odds with Galatians 4:21-31. Yet there is no discussion of this text.

Another observation relates to the book's hermeneutic. While he appears to be quite critical of dispensationalism, contending that its eschatology is a

Marcionite heresy (83), TMG appears to operate on a similar hermeneutical wavelength as dispensationalism. In general, a dispensational hermeneutic understands the promises of the OT to be fulfilled literally. Dispensationalists generally look at passages related to land in the OT and conclude that a future fulfillment awaits these promises before the second coming of Christ. In like manner, Boot seems to apply the same hermeneutical method. He understands the promise of land to be fulfilled in a material way before the return of Christ. This is especially highlighted in his discussion of the three land grants (73). For Boot, the kingdom is a matter of physical expansion, and the kingdom's expansion can be quantified by, among other things, the application and use of biblical law at the institutional level. Thus, to the degree that biblical laws are used in the courts, for example, is the degree that the kingdom of God is manifested.

Barring these observations, TMG also contains many errors of spelling, grammar, typography, and citation. Titles of books in the endnotes are inconsistent; some are italicized, others are in quotation marks, and the same works appear capitalized and then lowercased. Names are misspelled (e.g., J. S. Elliot, Schofield, Mathew). Semicolons occur very inconsistently, often used where a comma should be, thus creating incomplete sentences. The use of commas in lists is conflicting. Some lists employ the Oxford comma, but the majority do not. Quotation marks are sometimes absent (e.g., 201) and sometimes occur where they should not (e.g., block quotation on 503). There are multiple mistakes in Bible references, and, while the natural manner of presenting parenthetical lists of Bible references is linear, i.e., from Genesis to Revelation, the book's practice is erratic (see, e.g., 151).

When engaging with proponents of an opposing position, the work often employs genetic and *ad hominem* fallacies. In his discourse on utopia, Boot begins with a discussion of Jean Jacques Rousseau, whom he understands as the predecessor of Marxism. He does not reference Rousseau at all yet concludes that Rousseau is wrong because he is "odious," a "professional hypocrite," and "debauched narcissist" whose character is "infantile and vile" (157). Meredith Kline is refuted as "fanciful and excessively dependent on endless typologies," adopting a position that is "highly problematic" (321–322). Tim Keller is "confused," having produced a "confusing work" that "ties himself in knots." Boot claims to be discouraged because Keller "seems to have become overanxious to please the current culture and sound trendy" (204). Boot's response to *Generous Justice* includes the following observations: "contorted logic," "muddled caveats," and "anti-biblical." He further concludes that "Keller is simply talking nonsense" and that he "should simply know better" (213). In like manner, Boot attacks Horton for his two-kingdom perspective. Boot refers to two-kingdom adherents as "cowards" and "cultural retreatists" (381). Advocates of two kingdoms are indicted with "treason to the king of righteousness" because of "a doomed attempt to wed idolatry with true worship, righteousness with lawlessness" (384). These charges are laid within the first six pages of the two-kingdom critique, yet Horton is quoted only once. Carl Trueman also receives unjust criticism, being charged with "English snobbery" and forsaking objective historiography with "a visceral emotional outburst" (644 n. 1).

On the whole, TMG seems to be the product of someone who has legitimate concerns about the state of society. Unfortunately, the solutions to these concerns are not presented carefully, either from the Bible or from history. The number of errors is so significant that it should alarm readers to know that this book is in its second edition. Given its influence, pastors should read this work. A word of caution is in order, however. While the book may certainly resonate with many conservatives (like this reviewer) who see the West's social values as increasingly decaying, its rhetoric may overshadow its scholarly integrity. What we see in TMG is a hermeneutical method that oddly lines up with post-modernism, where historical and cultural observations are added to the process of text interpretation. Pastors seeking to be faithful in the interpretation of Scripture cannot allow culture to drive the process of exegesis.

www.ingramcontent.com/pod-product-compliance
Lightning Source LLC
Chambersburg PA
CBHW052105090426
42741CB00009B/1677